I0145756

# CAUSES AND PRINCIPLES IN ARABIC

# CAUSES AND PRINCIPLES IN ARABIC

Joyce Åkesson

Pallas Athena

Lund

2011

*Causes and Principles in Arabic*

All Rights Reserved

Copyright © 2011 by Joyce Åkesson

2011 Pallas Athena Distribution, Skarpskyttevägen 10 A, 226 42 Lund, Sweden.

Book design by Joyce Åkesson

This book may not be reproduced, stored in a retrieval system or transmitted in any form or by any means, electronic, mechanical, photocopying, recording, scanning or otherwise without the prior permission of the Publisher except in the case of brief quotations embodied in critical articles and reviews.

ISBN: 978-91-978954-3-9

PRINTED IN THE UNITED STATES OF AMERICA

ALSO BY JOYCE ÅKESSON

*A Study of Arabic Morphology,* Pallas Athena Distribution, August 2010.

*The Basics & Intricacies of Arabic Morphology,* Pallas Athena Distribution, July 2010.

*The Phonological Changes due to the Hamza and Weak Consonant in Arabic,* Pallas Athena Distribution, April 2010.

*A Study of the Assimilation and Substitution in Arabic,* Pallas Athena Distribution, March 2010.

*The Essentials of the Class of the Strong Verb in Arabic,* Pallas Athena Distribution, January 2010

*The Complexity of the Irregular Verbal and Nominal Forms & the Phonological Changes in Arabic,* Pallas Athena Distribution, April 2009.

*Arabic Morphology and Phonology:* Based on the Marāḥ al-Arwāḥ by Aḥmad b. ᶜAlī b. Masᶜūd, Studies in Semitic

Languages and Linguistics, Brill Academic Publishers, July 2001.

*Aḥmad B. ᶜAlī B. Masᶜūd on Arabic Morphology, Marāḥ al-Arwāḥ: Part 1: The Strong Verb,* Studia Orientalia Lundensia, Vol. 4, Brill Academic Publishers, October 1990.

*POETRY*

*Majnūn Leyla: Poems about Passion,* Pallas Athena Distribution, December 2009.

*The Invitation,* Pallas Athena Distribution, July 2009.

*Love's Thrilling Dimensions,* Pallas Athena Distribution, February 2009.

## TABLE OF CONTENTS

# PREFACE

One of the interesting features in Arabic linguistics is the reference to causes and principles in the explanation of many linguistic phenomena. This scientific approach seems to have developed from the middle of the $8^{th}$ century and onwards with the influence of Greek philosophy on Arabic linguistics and on other disciplines.

The present book provides information on several causes and principles in Arabic morphology and phonology, with a strong focus on the words, letters and vowels. Examples, qur'anic quotations and verses are presented in both Arabic script and Roman transcription and different theories are explored. Some of the causes that are discussed are the choice of a certain letter or vowel to a form, different phonological changes such as the elision or the addition of a vowel or a letter and the likes or dislikes of certain combinations. The references to several works of linguistics from the classical period until our days elucidate many intricacies and reflect the interests of several linguists in these topics.

# I. ABOUT A FEW WORDS

## 1- The frequency of usage of a word can be the reason of the elision of a letter in its structure

This cause has been mentioned by al-Māzinī. An example is the elison of the *y* that is the middle radical in the Form X of the perfect *ʾistaḥyaytu* إستحْيَيْتُ "I became shy" and the transfer of its fatḥa to the *ḥ,* namely *ʾistaḥaytu* إستحَيْتُ. This alleviation has been carried out due to the frequency of usage of this verb (cf. Ibn Ğinnī, *Munṣif II,* 204, Hindāwī, *Manāhiğ* 352).

Another example is *bi-smi l-lāhi* (without the *waṣla* before the s) بسمِ الله said instead of *bi-smi l-lāhi* (with the *waṣla* before the *s)* باسمِ الله "in the name of God".

## 2- Only nouns can be formed of five radicals and not verbs

An example of a noun with five radicals is *safarǧalun* سَفَرْجَلٌ "quince". Verbs cannot be formed of five radicals differently from nouns, which can be formed of five radicals without any prefix, infix or suffix. According to al-Māzinī, this is because the nouns are stronger than the verbs, as the nouns are not in need of verbs in the sentence whereas the verbs are in need of the nouns, and there does not exist at all a verb that is formed of five radicals (cf. Ibn Ǧinnī, *Munṣif I,* 28, Hindāwī, *Manāhiǧ* 354).

## 3- No noun occurs with a *w* at its extremity that is preceded by a letter vowelled with a ḍamma

The only exception to this rule is the personal pronoun of the masc. sing. *huwa* هُوَ "he" (cf. Åkesson, *Ibn Mas*ᶜ*ūd* fols. 5b-7a). The pronoun is counted to pertain to the same category as the noun, if one considers that the parts of the speech are three: noun, verb and particle.

The dislike of having the noun occuring with a *w* at its extremity that is preceded by a letter vowelled with a ḍamma is the reason why the plural of the noun *dalwun* دَلْوٌ "bucket" is made *ʾadlin* أدْلٍ (cf. Ibn Ǧinnī, *de Flexione* 43, Zamaḫšarī, 185, Ibn Yaᶜīš, X, 107-108, Ibn Mālik, *Alfīya* 147, Lane, I, 909, Wright, II, 209) and not *ʾadluwun* أدْلُوٌ.

However, the *w* can be found at the extremity of the verb, e.g. *yadᶜ(u)ū* يَدْعُو "he invites".

**4- The pronouns bring back the word to its original form**

As an example, *ḍarabtum(u)ūhu* ضَرَبْتُمُوهُ "you /masc. pl. hit him" can be taken up. The underlying *ū* in it is maintained between the pronoun of the nominative of the 2nd person of the masc. pl., *-tum,* and the pronoun of the accusative of the 3rd person of the sing. , the *-hu,* and thus the *u* is not longer at the extremity of the word, which is the reason why it is not elided. The base form of *ḍarabtum* ضَرَبْتُمْ is *ḍarabtum(u)ū* ضَرَبْتُمُوا, and the suffixed pronoun of the accusative, the *-hu,* is a reason why the verb is brought back to its base form (cf. Ibn Yaᶜīš, III, 95). The principle that the pronouns bring back the words to their base form can be considered a rule (cf. Sībawaihi, I, 341-342). The suffixed pronoun of the pl. of the 2nd person of the masc. pl., the *ū,* can be elided according to Yūnus referred to by Sībawaihi, I, 342, who accepts instead of the examples *ʾaᶜṭaytukum(u)ūhu* أعْطَيْتُكُمُوهُ "you /masc. pl. gave him" and ᵓaᶜṭaytukum(u)ūh(a)ā أَعْطَيْتُكُمُوهَا "you /masc. pl. gave her" ᵓaᶜṭaytukumhu أَعْطَيْتُكُمْهُ and ᵓaᶜṭaytukumh(a)ā أَعْطَيْتُكُمْهَا. Ibn Ǧinnī, *Sirr I,* 103 considers the saying of Yūnus of ᵓaᶜṭaytukumhu أَعْطَيْتُكُمْهُ to be an anomaly.

**5- The dual endings bring back the word to its original form**

The dual endings bring back the word to its original form. An example is the verb with 3rd radical *w* *daᶜaw(a)ā* دَعَوَا "they both invited /masc. sing." in which the *w* remains unchanged referring to the *w* of the root *d ᶜ w,* i.e. that it is not changed into an *ā,* like in the singular form *daᶜawa* دَعَوَ that becomes *daᶜ(a)ā* دَعَا "he invited" with final *alif mamdūda.* Another example is *ġazaw(a)ā* غَزَوَا "they both raided /masc. sing.".

An example of a verb with 3rd radical *y* is *ramay(a)ā* رَمَيَا "they both threw /masc. sing."

## II. ABOUT A FEW LETTERS AND VOWELS

### 6- The combination of the *y* and *w* is disliked

The combination of the *y* preceding the *w* is disliked. This is why the *y* as 2nd radical preceding the *w* as 3rd radical does not occur in in the doubly weak verbs.

The common conjugations of the doubly weak verbs are:

1- *faᶜala yafᶜilu* فَعَلَ يَفْعِلُ, e.g. *ṭawaya yaṭwiyu* طَوَيَ يَطْوِيُ that becomes after the phonological change *ṭaw(a)ā* طَوَى [with final *alif maqṣūra] yaṭw(i)ī* يَطْوِي "to fold".

2- *faᶜila yafᶜalu* فَعِلَ يَفْعَلُ (with 2nd radical *w* preceding 3rd radical (with 2nd radical *w* preceding 3rd radical *y),* e.g. *qawiya yaqwayu* قَوِيَ يَقْوَيُ "to be strong" of which only the imperfect becomes after the phonological change *yaqw(a)ā* [with final *alif maqṣūra]* يَقْوَى.

3- *fa<sup>c</sup>ila yaf<sup>c</sup>alu* فَعِلَ يَفْعَلُ (with 2nd radical *y* preceding 3rd radical *y),* e.g. *ḥayiya yaḥyayu* حَيِيَ يَحْيَيُ of which only the imperfect becomes after the phonological change *yaḥy(a)ā* [with final *alif mamdūda]* يَحْيَا.

#### 7- The *y* prefix occurs rarely in nouns

The *y* occurs very rarely as a prefix to nouns in Arabic and in some of the other Semitic languages (for examples see Wright, *Comparative Grammar* 182, Cohen, *Études* 34). It occurs in some nouns of animals, e.g. *yarḥ(u)ūmun* يَرْحُومٌ "male vulture", *ya<sup>c</sup>b(u)ūbun* يَعْبُوبٌ "horse", of plants, e.g. *ya<sup>c</sup>ḍ(i)īdun* يَعضِيدٌ "a kind of plant", and in a few adjectives, e.g. *yaḫḍ(i)īrun* يَخْضِيرٌ "green". These nominal forms could have derived from verbs in the 3rd person of the masc. sing. of the imperfect with some modifications (for examples and discussions see Cohen, *Études* 34).

**8- The *y* radical as an initial letter vowelled by a fatḥa is considered as heavy in nouns**

The *y* radical vowelled by a fatḥa is also considered as heavy in the nouns, which is why it is sometimes substituted by a hamza. An example is *yadayhi* يَدَيْهِ "both his hands" which is said as *ᵓadayhi* أَدَيْهِ (cf. Ibn ᶜUṣfūr, I, 346-347, Zamaḫšarī, 173, Ibn Yaᶜīš, X, 15, Ibn Manẓūr, VI, 4951, Åkesson, *Ibn Masᶜūd,* the Commentary (324), Vernier, I, 346, Howell, IV, fasc. I, 1231) with this substitution.

Another example is *yalalun* يَلَلٌ "a shortness of the upper teeth" which is said as *ᵓalalun* أَلَلٌ with this particular substitution of the hamza for the initial *y* vowelled by a fatḥa.

**9- The *w* is disliked as the 1st initial letter in nouns**

The *w* that is vowelled with a fatḥa can be changed into a hamza due to this dislike, e.g. *waw(a)āṣilu* وَوَاصِلُ the pl. of *w(a)āṣilatun* وَاصِلَةٌ "joining" becomes *ᵓaw(a)āṣilu* أَوَاصِلُ and *waw(a)āqin* وَوَاقٍ, the pl. of *w(a)āqiyatun* وَاقِيَةٌ "preserver", becomes *ᵓaw(a)āqin* أَوَاقٍ (cf. Zamaḫšarī, 172, Ibn Yaᶜīš, X, 10,

Ibn ᶜAqīl, II, 552, Åkesson, *Ibn Masᶜūd,* the Commentary (316)). The diminutive *wuzayzatun* وُزَيْزَةٌ "little goose" of *wazzatun* وَزَّةٌ "goose" can become *ᵓuzayzatun* أُزَيْزَةٌ (cf. Ibn Ǧinnī, *Munṣif I,* 112-113).

The *w* that is vowelled with a ḍamma has a tendency to be changed into a hamza. An example is the original form *wuǧ(u)ūhun* وُجُوهٌ that becomes *ᵓuǧ(u)ūhun* أُجُوهٌ "faces" (cf. Sībawaihi, II, 341, Ibn Ǧinnī, *de Flexione* 25, Sirr I, 92, Ibn ᶜUṣfūr, I, 332, Zamaḫšarī, 172, Ibn Yaᶜīš, X, 10-11, Howell, IV, fasc. I, 1224-1225, Åkesson, *Ibn Masᶜūd,* the Commentary (321)), which is the pl. of *waǧhun* وَجْهٌ "face". Another example with this substitution carried out is *wuqqitat* وُقِّتَتْ which becomes *ᵓuqqitat* أُقِّتَتْ "appointed a time" (cf. Ibn Ǧinnī, *Munṣif I,* 112-113). It occurs in the sur. 77: 11 *(wa-ᵓiḏā ᵓuqqitati r-rusulu)* وَإذَا أُقِّتَتِ الرُّسُلُ "And when the apostles are (all) appointed a time (to collect); -". It is however anomalously read with *wuqqitati* وُقِّتَتِ instead by Abū ᶜAmr whereas the remaining six readers read it with *ᵓuqqitati* أُقِّتَتِ (cf. Ibn Ḫālawaihi, *Qirāᵓāt II,* 428).

The *w* that is vowelled with a kasra has a tendency to be changed into a hamza. Examples are *wis(a)ādatun* وِسَادَةٌ that becomes *ʾis(a)ādatun* "cushion" إِسَادَةٌ and *wif(a)ādatun* وِفَادَةٌ that becomes *ʾif(a)ādatun* إِفَادَةٌ "embassy" (cf. Ibn Ǧinnī, *Munṣif I,* 112-113, Åkesson, *Ibn Masᶜūd,* the Commentary (322).

**10- The heavy *w* is chosen for the rarely used masc. pl. and the light *ā* for the frequently used dual in nouns**

A question of interest is why was the *ā* chosen to mark the dual, e.g. *muᶜallim(a)āni* مُعَلِّمَانِ "two teachers /masc. pl" and the *ū* chosen to mark the sound masc. pl. *muᶜallim(u)ūna* مُعَلِّمُونَ "teachers" in nouns occurring in the nominative. According to Ibn Ǧinnī, *Taṯniya* 70-72, the dual is more frequently used than the masc. sound pl., because not all nouns can have a masc. sound pl. Some have a broken pl. and others have a fem. pl. with the ending *-āt.* So the light *ā* was chosen for the frequently used dual and the heavy *ū* for the rarely used pl., so that what is deemed as heavy becomes rarely used and what is deemed as light becomes frequently used in the language.

According to Abū ᶜAlī referred to by Ibn Ǧinnī, *Taṯniya* 72, the pl. is stronger than the dual as it refers to different numbers whereas the dual refers only to two. For this reason the *w*, which is stronger than the *ā*, was chosen to mark the pl. that is stronger than the dual (for discussions see Zaǧǧāǧī, *Īḍāḥ* 121-129, Versteegh, *Zaǧǧāǧī* 216-230).

**11- The ending –ūna has been chosen to mark the masc. pl. of the imperfect of the indicative and the ending -āni to mark the dual**

The ending -*ūna* has been chosen to mark the masc. pl. of the imperfect of the indicative, e.g. *yaḍrib(u)ūna* يَضْرِبُونَ "they hit /masc. pl." and the ending -*āni* to mark the dual, e.g. *yaḍrib(a)āni* يَضْرِبَانِ "they hit /masc. dual" and *taḍrib(a)āni* تَضْرِبَانِ "they hit /fem. dual". It can be remarked that they are the same as those that mark the sound pl. and the dual respectively of nouns occurring in the nominative, e.g. *muᶜallim(u)ūna* مُعَلِّمُونَ "teachers", *muᶜallim(a)āni* مُعَلِّمَانِ "two teachers". The reason why they were chosen to be attached to the imperfect is the similarity between the imperfect and the noun (for it see Åkesson, *Ibn Mas*$^{c}$*ūd,* the Commentary (93)).

**12- The *alif mamdūda* is suffixed after the *ū* of the pl. in the 3rd person of the masc. pl. of the jussive**

The *alif mamdūda* suffixed after the *ū* of the pl. is termed as *alif al-wiqāya* "the guarding alif" (cf. Wright, I, 11). There exist different opinions concerning its occurrence.

According to al-Farrā$^{\circ}$'s theory, this alif is suffixed after the -*ū* of the pl., so that it is possible to differentiate between the *ū* which is a radical in verbs with 3rd weak radical and the *ū* marking the pl. As an example of a verb in the sing. ending with a *w* radical, *yad(u)*$^{c}$*ū* يَدْعُو "he calls" can be mentioned, and as an example of a verb in the jussive ending with the suffixed pronoun of the nominative of the masc. pl., the *ū,* preceding the *alif mamdūda, lam yad(u)*$^{c}$*ū* لم يَدْعُوا "they did not call" can be mentioned. Had it not been for the *alif madmdūda,* then both the singular and the pl. would be mixed together.

Some Arabs use defectively the indicative mood of the sing. in some cases of weak 3rd radical verbs instead of the correct jussive mood (for a study of such cases see Zamaḫšarī, 184-185, Ibn Yaᶜīš, X, 104-107, Wright, IV 389) by maintaining the 3rd weak radical instead of eliding it. An example is *lam yadᶜ(u)ū* لم يَدْعُو "he did not call" with the maintainance of the *ū* said instead of the correct *lam yadᶜu* (cf. Åkesson, *Ibn Masᶜūd,* fol. 5a) with its elision. Had it not been for the *alif mamdūda* after the *ū,* then both the sing., i.e. *lam yadᶜū* لم يَدْعُو "he did not call" in this defective dialectal variant, and the pl., i.e. *lam yadᶜ(u)ū* لم يَدْعُوا (with the *alif mamdūda* after the *ū)* "they did not call" would have been mixed up together.

This defective maintainance of the *ū* in the jussive occurs in this verse said by an unknown poet, cited by Zamaḫšarī, 184, Ibn Yaᶜīš, X, 104, Howell, IV, fasc. I, 1576 and Wright, IV 389, in which *lam tahğ(u)ū* لم تَهْجُو occurs instead of *lam tahğu* لم تَهْجُ:

"هَجَوْتَ زَبّانَ ثُمّ جِئْتَ مُعتَذِرا مِنْ هَجْوِ زَبّانَ لم تَهْجُو ولم تَدَعِ".

*"hağawta Zabbāna ṯumma ği'ta mu'taḏiran*
*min hağwi Zabbāna lam tahğū wa-lam tada'i".*
"You did satirize Zabbān: then you came, apologizing
for satirizing Zabbān: you did not satirize [him], nor did
you leave [him] alone".

According to the theory of al-Aḫfaš, the alif is suffixed so that the wāw of the pl. is not mixed up with the wāw of the conjunction (cf. ᶜAbd al-Tawwāb's note on Rāzī, in Ḫalīl b. Aḥmad ..., *Ḥurūf* 135). An example is the phrase *ḥḍrwtkllm* حضروتكلم (cf. Åkesson, *Ibn Masᶜūd* 54: fol. 5a) written without diatritic signs and without an alif after the *w*. It can be read in two manners: *ḥaḍara wa-takallama* حَضَرَ وَتَكَلَّمَ "He came and talked" or *ḥaḍar(u)ū takallama* حَضَرُو تَكَلَّمَ "they came, he talked" causing an inevitable confusion, which is why the presence or the absence of the alif after the *w* is significant.

**13- The *t*, and not the *y*, was chosen as an imperfect prefix for the 3rd person of the fem. sing.**

The reasons why the *t*, and not the *y*, was chosen as an imperfect prefix for the 3rd person of the fem. sing. e.g. *taḍribu*

تَضْرِبُ "she hits, fem. sing." - and not *yaḍribu* يَضْرِبُ as with the 3rd person of the masc. sing. - is on the one hand to avoid confusing it with the masc. sing. *yaḍribu* يَضْرِبُ "he hits", and on the other, to conform this *t* with the *t* that is chosen as a suffix that marks the fem. sing. in the perfect (cf. Wright, *Comparative Grammar* 184), i.e. *ḍarabat* ضَرَبَتْ "she hit" (cf. Åkesson, *Ibn Mas*ᶜ*ūd,* the Commentary (97)).

**14- The *y* and not the *t* was chosen as an imperfect prefix for the 3rd person of the fem. pl.**

The *y,* and not the *t,* was chosen as an imperfect prefix for the 3rd person of the fem. pl., e,g. *yaḍribna* يَضْرِبْنَ "they hit /fem. pl." - and not *taḍribna* تَضْرِبْنَ, to avoid the combination of two markers of the fem.: the *t* prefix of the fem. and the *n* suffix of he fem. if the *t* was to be chosen instead. An exception to this rule is the anomalous reading *tatafaṭṭarna* تَتَفَطَّرْنَ of the sur. 42: 5 which has been recorded instead of the correct form *yatafaṭṭarna* يَتَفَطَّرْنَ "Rent asunder" (cf. Wright, II, 56, *Comparative Grammar* 185, Åkesson, *Ibn Mas*ᶜ*ūd,* the Commentary (97)). The prefixation of the *t* in this example is due probably to a false analogy with the 3rd person of the fem. sing.

**15- The *y* is chosen in the ending *-īna* for the 2nd person of the fem. sing. of the imperfect of the indicative**

The reason why the *ī* is chosen as an infix in *taḍrib(i)īna* تَضْرِبِينَ "you hit /fem.sing." and not the *t,* is that the prefixed *t* of the addressed 2nd person prohibited this infixation, as this would imply a disliked repetion of two tā°s if *taḍributna* تَضْرِبُتْنَ is said instead (cf. Åkesson, *Ibn Mas°ūd,* the Commentary (88)).

Furthermore, the choice of the *-ī* infix in this form that is specific for the fem. is justified by Ibn Mas°ūd (Åkesson, *Ibn Mas°ūd* 62: fol. 8b) who compares it with the *-ī* that replaces the *-hi* that marks the fem. sing. in the demonstratif pronoun *h(a)āḏihi* هَذِهِ which becomes *hāḏ(i)ī* هَذِي in the expression *hāḏī ᵓamatu l-lāhi* هَذِي أَمَةُ اللّه "this is God's maid-servant" (for this substitution see Rāzī, in Ḫalīl b. Aḥmad ..., *Ḥurūf* 154, Sībawaihi, II, 341, Ibn Ǧinnī, *Sirr II,* 556, Zamaḫšarī, 176).

This substitution implies a closeness between the *hi* and the *ī* in marking the feminization and makes the *-ī* fit to be a marker of the fem. Furthermore, the *-ī* infix is necessary so that the sing. form *taf<sup>c</sup>al(i)īna* تَفْعَلِينَ would be distinguished from the pl. form of the fem. *taf<sup>c</sup>alna* تَفْعَلْنَ "you do /fem. pl." (cf. Åkesson, *Ibn Mas<sup>c</sup>ūd* 62: fol. 8b).

**16- The *m* has the characteristic of only being added to the noun and pronoun**

The *m* can be found as infixed in a pronoun, e.g. *ʾantum(a)ā* أَنْتُمَا "you two", or suffixed in it, e.g. *ʾantum* أَنْتُمْ "you /masc. pl.". It is prefixed in nouns (for discussions see Fleisch, *Traité I,* 422-434), e.g. *maw<sup>c</sup>idun* مَوْعِدٌ "a place of a promise or an appointment" or suffixed to them (for discussions see ibid, 465-467), e.g. *ʾibnum* إِبْنُمْ meaning *al-ʾibnu* الإِبْنُ "the son" in which it marks intensification (cf. Zağğāğī, *Mağālis* 134). It is not to be prefixed, infixed or suffixed directly in verbs (cf. Ibn Ya<sup>c</sup>īš, *Mulūkī* 150). It can be noted that in the cases of the 2nd persons of the masc. and fem. dual and the masc. pl. of the perfect, e.g. *ḍarabtum(a)ā* ضَرَبْتُمَا "you hit /masc. and fem. dual" and *ḍarabtum* ضَرَبْتُمْ "you hit /masc. pl.", the *m* is a part of the suffixed pronouns *–tum(a)ā* تُمَا and *–tum* تُمْ. (cf. Åkesson, *Ibn Mas<sup>c</sup>ūd,* the Commentary (62).

*16.1 Anomalous cases:*

In some anomalous cases of verbs the *m* can be prefixed or infixed (for examples see Ibn Ǧinnī, *Sirr I,* 432-433). These forms are *tamaf<sup>c</sup>ala* تمفْعَل and *maf<sup>c</sup>ala* مَفْعَلَ.

Examples conformale to *tamaf<sup>c</sup>ala* تَمَفْعَلَ are: .g. *tamaskana l-rağulu* تَمَسكَنَ الرّجُلُ "the man became poor", e.g. *tamadra<sup>c</sup>a* تَمَدْرَعَ "he wore a loose outer garment of wool with sleeves, slit in front", *tamandala* تَمَنْدَلَ "to clean oneself with a handkerchief", *tamanṭaqa* تَمَنْطَقَ "to tighten one's belt", *tamaslama l-rağulu* تَمَسلَمَ الرّجُلُ "the man named himself Muslim" and *tamawl(a)ā* تَمَوْلَى "to behave arrogantly".

Examples conformale to *maf<sup>c</sup>ala* مَفْعَلَ are: *marḥabaka l-lāhu wamashalaka* مَرْحَبَكَ اللّهُ وَمَسهَلَكَ "may God welcome you and make the place smooth, plain, or not rugged for you", and *maḫraqa l-rağulu* مَخْرَقَ الرَّجُلُ "the man was profuse in liberality, bounty, or munificence".

**17- Two markers should not be combined together**

*17.1 The –na that marks the fem. should not be combined with the doubled n:*

The *ā* is inserted before the double *n* in *li-yaḍribn(a)ānni* لِيَضْرِبْنَانِّي "let them hit! /fem. pl." that is said instead of *li-yaḍribnanni* لِيَضْرِبْنَنِّي to avoid the combination of the *-na* that marks the fem., namely in *li-yaḍribna* لِيَضْرِبْنَ with the doubled *n* (cf. Sībawaihi, II, 160, Ibn ᶜAqīl, II, 316, Åkesson, *Ibn Masᶜūd,* the Commentary (128)).

*17.2 The –na that is a declinable marker of the indicative should not be combined with the doubled n that is an undeclinable marker:*

The imperfect, Energetic I, of the masc. dual *yaḍrib(a)ānni* يَضْرِبَانِّي "they hit /3 masc. dual" is underlyingly *yaḍrib(a)ānanni*

يَضْرِبَانِّنِي, in which the 1st *n,* which is the *-na* of the indicative marking the declension, is elided as it is combined with the doubled *n* that is undeclinable. The reason of this elision is to avoid the combination of a declinable marker with an undeclinable one (Åkesson, *Ibn Mas*$^{c}$*ūd,* the Commentary (127)).

*17.3 Two markers of the fem. should not be combined together in the heavy verb:*

This dislike of combining two markers of the fem. in the verb is noticed in the case of the perfect of the 3rd person of the fem. pl. *ḍarabna* ضَرَبْنَ underlyingly *ḍarabatna* ضَرَبَتْنَ (for discussions see Åkesson, *Ibn Mas*$^{c}$*ūd,* the Commentary (58)) and in the case of the imperfect of the 3rd person of the fem. pl. *yaḍribna* يَضْرِبْنَ "they hit /fem. pl." in which the *y* was chosen as a prefix and not the *t* characteristic for the fem. (cf. ibid, (97)).

*17.4 Two identical markers should not be combined in the noun:*

Examples are nouns in the fem. sing. with final *t marbūṭa* that are put in the plural by suffixing the ending *–āt* ات to them, e.g.

*muslimatun* مُسْلِمَةٌ "a muslim girl or woman" which becomes *muslim(a)ātun* مُسْلِمَاتٌ originally *muslimat(a)ātun* مُسْلِمَتَاتٌ.

The reason of eliding one of both the tā°s of the fem. is the heaviness implied by the combination of two letters of the same kind together (cf. Ibn Ǧinnī, *Ḫaṣā°iṣ III,* 235, Ibn al-Anbārī, *Inṣāf* Q. 4, 20, Åkesson, *Ibn Mas°ūd,* the Commentary (58)).

**18- Two different markers of the fem. can be combined together in the light noun, as by principle nouns are lighter than verbs**

The *alif maqṣūra* that marks the fem. in *ḥubl(a)ā* (with final *alif maqṣūra)* حُبْلَى "pregnant woman" is allowed to be combined with the *t* that marks the fem. pl. of the ending *-ātun* after that this alif is changed into a *y,* i.e. *ḥublay(a)ātun* حُبْلَيَاتٌ (cf. Zamaḫšarī, 79, Ibn Ya°īš, V, 61-62, Wright, II, 192, 197), because both the *y* and the *t* are different letters. The *alif maqṣūra's* change into a *y* vowelled by a fatḥa occurs necessarily to avoid the cluster of two vowelless letters, the vowelless *alif maqṣūra* and the vowelless *ā* of the fem. pl. ending *-ātun,* i.e. *ḥubl(a)āātun* حُبْلاات becomes *ḥublay(a)ātun*

حُبْلَيَاتٌ. There is no heaviness implied by the combination of both these markers of the fem. when it takes place in the noun contrarily to if it was to occur in the verb, e.g. *yaḍribna* يَضْرِبْنَ "they hit /fem. pl." that occurs instead of *taḍribna* تَضْرِبْنَ, as by principle, nouns are lighter than verbs (cf. Åkeson, Ibn *Mas*ᶜ*ūd,* the Commentary (58)).

An anomalous case is the anomalous reading *tatafaṭṭarna* تَتَفَطّرْنَ of the sur. 42: 5 which has been recorded instead of the correct form *yatafaṭṭarna* يَتَفَطّرْنَ "Rent asunder" (cf. Wright, II, 56, *Comparative Grammar* 185). The prefixation of the *t* in this example is due probably to a false analogy with the 3rd person of the fem. sing.

**19- The marker should not be elided**

According to a general principle, the marker should not be elided (cf. Ḥassān, *Uṣūl* 142).

For instance, in verbs of Form V *tatafa*ᶜᶜ*alu* تَتَفَعّلُ and VI *tatafā*ᶜ*alu* تَتَفَاعَلُ that occur in the 2nd person of the fem. and the 3rd person of the masc. sing. of the imperfect, e.g. *tataqalladu*

تَتَقَلّدُ "you assume /masc. sing." and "/3 fem. sing." and *tatabā*ᶜ*adu* تَتَبَاعَدُ "you move away or she moves away", two tā°s are combined together. The 1st one is the imperfect prefix and the 2nd is the marker of reflexivity. The repetition of the tā°s is considered as heavy by some who prefer to elide one of them for the sake of alleviation (for a study of this particular elision see Howell, IV, fasc. II, 1822-1828, de Sacy, I, 221, Wright, II, 65, Vernier, I, 346). Thus *tataqalladu* تَتَقَلّدُ becomes *taqalladu* تَقَلّدُ after the elision and *tatabā*ᶜ*adu* تَتَبَاعَدُ becomes *tabā*ᶜ*adu* تَبَاعَدُ. Sībawaihi, II, 475-476 and the Basrans believe that the 2nd *t* that marks the reflexivity is more fit to be elided, because the 1st one is more important as it is the prefix marking the imperfect. The Kufans however believe that it is the 1st *t* that should be elided because the 2nd one marks the reflexivity whereas the 1st one is prefixed and its elision is easier (for the debate see Ibn al-Anbārī, *Inṣāf* Q. 93, 269-271).

**20- The elision of the added segment is more prior than the elision of a radical**

This is the case of the passive participle form *maf*ᶜ*uwlun* / *maf*ᶜ*(u)ūlun* مَفْعُولٌ, e.g. *maqwuwlun* / *maqw(u)ūlun* مَقْوُولٌ "what is said". The first step of the phonological change is that the ḍamma of the 2nd radical *w* is shifted to the vowelless segment preceding it (cf. Åkesson, *Ibn Mas$^c$ūd* 292: fol. 31a). Thus *maqw(u)ūlun* with the 2nd radical *w* vowelled by a ḍamma and preceded by a sukūn becomes *maquwūlun* مَقُوْوُلٌ after that the *w's* ḍamma is shifted to the *q*.

According to the theory of Sībawaihi, *maquwūlun* مَقُوْوُلٌ which presents a cluster of two vowelless wāws, the *w* preceded by a ḍamma and the *ū,* becomes *maquwlun* مَقُوْلٌ after that the infixed wāw, i.e. the *ū,* is elided. According to him, *maquwlun* مَقُوْلٌ is formed according to the pattern *mafu$^c$lun* مَفُعْلٌ. As the vowelless *w* is preceded by a ḍamma, the *w* is changed into an *ū* so that it becomes *maq(u)ūlun* مقُولٌ.

According to Sībawaihi it is the infixed wāw: the *ū,* that is elided from *maquwūlun* مَقُوْوُلٌ on account of the principle that the elision of the added segment, - by which he means the infixed *w* in this form -, is more prior than the elision of a radical.

**21- Four vowelled letters cannot follow each other in one word**

According to a common principle, four vowelled letters cannot follow each other in one word (cf. Zaǧǧāǧī, *Īḍāḥ* 75, Ibn Ǧinnī, *Sirr I,* 220-221, Ḥassān, *Uṣūl* 228, Åkesson, *Ibn Masᶜūd,* the Commentary (55)).

Hence, the 3rd radical is made vowelless in the perfect verb when the pronoun of the nominative is suffixed to it, e.g. *ḍarabna* ضَرِبْنَ "they hit, /fem. pl.", *ḍarbtu* ضَرِبْتُ "I hit", *ḍarabta* ضَرِبْتَ "you hit, /masc. sing." and *ḍarabti* ضَرِبْتِ "you hit /fem. sing." in order to avoid the disliked succession of vowels.

It is also made vowelless in the case of the imperfect and imperative when the vowelled agent suffix pronoun, the –*na* of the fem. pl., is attached to it, e.g. the imperfect *taḍribna* تَضْرِبْنَ "you hit /fem. pl." and the imperative *ʾiḍribna* إِضْرِبْنَ "hit! /fem.pl." and the imperfect *yaḍribna* يَضْرِبْنَ "they hit /fem. pl.".

<u>21.1 The case of the doubled verb:</u>

The assimilation is forbidden in the forms of the doubled verb occurring in the perfect, imperfect and imperative in which the vowelled agent pronouns are suffixed to, in order to avoid the disliked combination of the four vowels. Hence the forms implied for instance by the example *madada* مَدَدَ "to stretch" are: *madadtu* مَدَدْتُ, *madadta* مَدَدْتَ, *madadti* مَدَدْتِ, *madadn(a)ā* مَدَدْنَا, *madadtum* مَدَدْتُمْ, *madadtunna* مَدَدْتُنَّ and *madadna* مَدَدْنَ which all occur with the elision of the fatḥa from the 2nd *d* of *madada* مَدَدَ.

As well, no assimilation occurs in the 2nd and 3rd person of the fem. pl. in the case of the imperfect, namely *tamdudna* تَمْدُدْنَ "you stretch /fem. pl." and *yamdudna* يَمْدُدْنَ "they stretch /fem. pl." respectively, and in the case of the 2nd person of the fem. pl. of the imperative, namely *ʾumdudna* أُمْدُدْنَ "stretch!".

The elision of one of the identical letters is a possibility in some anomalous cases.

An example is the perfect of the 2nd person of the masc. sing. *ẓalilta* ظَلِلْتَ "you continued all day" and of the 2nd person of the fem. sing. *ẓalilti* ظَلِلْتِ that becomes after the elision of one of the lāms *ẓalta* ظَلْتَ and *ẓalti* ظَلْتِ respectively (cf. Ibn Mālik, *La Alfīya* 222, Ibn ᶜAqīl, II, 584, Åkesson, *Ibn Masᶜūd* 196: fol. 18b, Wright, II, 69, Howell, IV, fasc. II, 1836 sqq., de Sacy, I, 228). The alleviated form *ẓalta* ظَلْتَ occurs in the sur. 20: 97 *(l-laḏī ẓalta ᶜalayhi ᶜākifan)* ألّذي ظَلْتَ عَلَيْهِ عاكفا "Of whom thou hast become a devoted worshipper", and *ẓaltum* ظَلْتُمْ in the sur. 56: 65 *(fa-ẓaltum tafakkahūna)* فَظَلْتُمْ تَفَكَّهُونَ "And ye would be left in wonderment" (cf. Howell, IV, fasc. II, 1836).

It can be remarked that in the dialectal variant of the Banū ᶜĀmir, the 2nd radical *l* of the perfect of the 1st person of the sing. *ẓaliltu* ظَلِلْتُ is elided, and the fatḥa which is the vowelling of the 1st radical remains unchanged, namely *ẓaltu* ظَلْتُ, whereas in the dialect of the Ḥiğāzīs the 2nd radical is elided after that its kasra is shifted to the 1st radical, namely *ẓiltu* ظِلْتُ (cf. ᶜAbd al-Ḥamīd, *Taṣrīf* 611, Talmon, *ᶜAyn* 184).

Concerning the variant *ẓaltu* ظَلْتُ, Sībawaihi, II, 446 notes that they compared it to *lastu* لَسْتُ "I am not". Both *ẓiltu* ظِلْتُ and *ẓaltu* ظَلْتُ can occur in this verse said by ᶜUmar b. Abī Rabīᶜa al-Maḫzūmi, cited by ᶜAbd al-Ḥamīd, *Taṣrīf* 611 in the note:

"ظِلْتُ فِيهَا ذَاتَ يَومَ وَاقِفًا أَسْأَلُ الْمَنْزِلَ هَلْ فِيهِ خَبَرْ؟".

*"Ẓiltu fīhā ḏāta yawma wāqifan*
*ᵓasᵓalu l-manzila hal fīhi ḫabar?".*
"And this day I remained standing by it,
asking the house if it had any news".

Both *ẓiltu* ظِلْتُ or *ẓaltu* ظَلْتُ with the elision of the *l* and *maliltu* مَلِلْتُ with its maintainance are combined in this verse said by ᶜUmar b. Abī Rabīᶜa, cited by ᶜAbd al-Ḥamīd, *Taṣrīf* 611 in the note:

"وَمَا مَلِلْتُ وَلَكِنْ زَادَ حُبُّكُم وَمَا ذَكَرْتُكِ إِلاَّ ظَلْتُ كَالسَدِرِ".

*"Wa-mā maliltu wa-lākin zāda ḥubbukum*
*wamā ḏakartuki ᵓillā ẓiltu (/ẓaltu] ka-l-sadiri".*
"I did not become weary but my love for you has

increased.

Whenever I think of you I become as the possessed".

Another example is the imperative of the 2nd person of the pl. *ᵓiqrirna* اِقْرِرْنَ "stay quietly!" that becomes after the elision of one of the rāᵓs *qirna* قِرْنَ. *ᵓiqrirna* اِقْرِرْنَ is from the root *q r r* with 2nd and 3rd radical *r* (cf. Ibn Manẓūr, V, 3578-3579), in which the 2nd *r* is vowelless on the basis that the sukūn marks the imperative and that the vowelled agent pronoun is suffixed to it. The sequence of the identical segments in *ᵓiqrirna* اِقْرِرْنَ is that of a vowelled segment, namely the 2nd radical *r,* preceding a vowelless segment, namely the 3rd radical *r,* which by principle should prevent the assimilation. The elision of the 1st *r* of the sequence is however a possibility after that its vowel is shifted to the *q,* and then the hamza of the imperative is also elided as it is not more needed now that the 1st radical *q* is vowelled. The resulting alleviated form is *qirna* قِرْنَ (cf. Ibn ᶜAqīl, II, 584-585, Åkesson, *Ibn Masᶜūd* 196: fol. 18b, Penrice, *Dictionary* 116).

The variant *qarna* قَرْنَ exists as well which pertains to another dialectal variant, and its base form is then the variant *ᵓiqrarna* اِقْرَرْنَ. It can be mentioned that *wa-qarna* وَقَرْنَ occurs instead of *wa-qirna* وقِرن in the sur. 33: 33 وَقَرْنَ في بُيُوتِكُنّ *(wa-qarna fī buyūtikunna)* and that it is the reading of Nāfi[c] and [c]Āṣim (cf. Ibn [c]Aqīl, II, 585).

<u>*21.2 The occurrence of the disliked combination of the four vowelled letters:*</u>

The case of the imperfect verb in which the 3rd radical is given a fatḥa when the pronoun of the accusative is suffixed to it can be mentioned, e.g. *ḍarabaka* ضَرَبَكَ "he hit you/masc. sing.", thus allowing the disliked combination of four vowelled letters. This case can be contrasted to the cases of the perfect, imperfect, and imperative in which the 3rd radical is made vowelless when the vowelled pronoun of the nominative is suffixed to it, e.g. *ḍarabta* ضَرَبْتَ "you hit /masc. sing.", *yaḍribna* يَضْرِبْنَ "they hit /fem. pl." and *ʾiḍribna* إضْرِبْنَ "hit! /fem. pl.".

In spite of the fact that the attached pronouns of the nominative and of the accusative are suffixed to the verb, the suffixed pronoun of the nominative is considered by the Arab grammarians as one with its verb, whereas the pronoun of the accusative is regarded as another word separated from it, thus leading to a proper rule as the acceptance of the succession of the four vowels. The verb is in need of an agent, manifest or suppressed, which is why it is considered as one with its pronoun of the agent, whereas it can manage without an object, which is the reason why it and its pronoun of the object are considered as two separate words (cf. Ibn Ǧinnī, *Sirr I,* 221).

*21.3 Cases in which the succession of four vowelled letters occurs in nouns:*

Examples are *hudabidun* هُدَبِدٌ originally *hudābidun* هُدَابِدٌ and *ᶜulabiṭun* عُلَبِطٌ originally *ᶜulābiṭun* عُلابِطٌ, both having their *ā* elided. There is a disliked succession of the four vowels that occurs in both these abbreviated forms (cf. Sībawaihi, II, 366).

A similar case with the four consecutive vowels that occur in one word is found in *ᶜaratunun* عَرَتُنٌ "a plant used in dyeing" conformable with *faᶜalulun* originally *ᶜarantunun* عَرَنْتُنٌ, in which the *n* is elided (cf. Ibn Manẓūr, IV, 2869), and *ǧanadilun* جَنَدِلٌ "stones" conformable with *faᶜalilun* originally *ǧanādilu* جَنَادِلُ in which a contraction is carried out (cf. Ibn Manẓūr, I,

699; for discussions see Ibn Ǧinnī, *Ḫaṣāʾiṣ* III, 114, Ibn Yaᶜīš, VI, 136).

**22- A vowelless letter is not a sufficient separative between two vowelled letters**

The vowelless letter that occurs between two vowelled letters is not a sufficient separative between two vowels or between two weak letters whose combination is disliked, to be able to hinder the change of one into the other. This is a principle which is taken into consideration (cf. Ḥassān, *Uṣūl* 217, Ibn al-Anbārī, *Inṣāf* Q. 118, 343, Åkesson, *Ibn Masūd,* the Introduction).

The *w* of the original form *qinwatu* قِنْوَةٌ is changed into a *y* (cf. Ibn Ǧinnī, *Ḫaṣāʾiṣ* I, 93, Ibn Manẓūr, V, 3759, Åkesson, *Ibn Masūd,* the Commentary (113)), resulting in *qinyatun* قِنْيَةٌ on account of the influence of the kasra of the *q*. In spite of the fact that the *n* is separating both the *qi* and the *wa,* its sukūn renders it too weak to stop the influence of the kasra preceding the *w* by two letters, which is the reason why the *w* is changed into the *y* in order to agree with the kasra. It can be noted that in some cases, the Ḥiğāzi dialect has a *y* and kasra against Eastern *w* and ḍamma, e.g. *qinyatun* قِنْيَةٌ and *miṣḥafun* مِصْحَفٌ "a codex" against *qinwatun* قِنْوَةٌ and *muṣḥafun* مُصْحَفٌ by the people of Tamīm (cf. Rabin, 101).

The sequence in the active participles with 2nd weak *w* *q(a)āwilun* قَاوِلٌ "sayer" and 2nd weak *y* *b(a)āyiᶜun* بَايِعٌ "seller" is that of a vowelled weak letter preceded by a fatḥa. In spite of the fact that there exists an *ā* between the vowelled *w* of *q(a)āwilun* قَاوِلٌ and the vowelled *y* of *b(a)āyiᶜun* بَايِعٌ, this *ā* is not taken into account as it is vowelless and occurs between two vowelled letters. So the vowelled *w* is changed into an *ā* due to the influence of the fatḥa preceding it, i.e. *q(a)āālun* قَاالٌ. The reason why one of the alifs is not dropped resulting in *q(a)ālun* قَالٌ is to prevent that the active participle is mixed up with the perfect *q(a)āla* قَالَ "he said" in the representation. The 2nd ā in *q(a)āālun* قَاالٌ is therefore changed into a hamza, i.e. *q(a)āᵓilun* قَائِلٌ to prevent the combination of two vowelless alifs (cf. for discussions Åkesson, *Ibn Masᶜūd,* the Commentary (290)).

The same happens with *b(a)āyiᶜun* بَايِعٌ that becomes *b(a)āāᶜun* بَااعٌ and then *b(a)āᵓiᶜun* بَائِعٌ " a seller".

Another example in which the vowelless *ā* is not taken into account is *kis(a)āwun* كَسَاوٌ “a wrapper”, in which the vowelled *w* is also changed into an *ā* due to the influence of the fatḥa preceding it, i.e. *kis(a)āā* كَساا. Then the *ā* is changed into a hamza to prevent the cluster of two vowelless alifs and the result is *kis(a)āʾun* كَساءٌ (cf. ibid).

In some cases of active participles with 2nd weak radical, the radical is elided (cf. ibid 290-292: fol. 30b). Some examples are *h(a)āᶜun* هَاعٌ "vomitting" used instead of *h(a)āʾiᶜun* هَائعٌ underlyingly *h(a)āwiᶜun* هَاوِعٌ from *hawaᶜa* هَوَعَ "to vomit", *l(a)āᶜun* لاعٌ "suffering" used instead of *l(a)āʾiᶜun* لائعٌ underlyingly *l(a)āwiᶜun* لاوِعٌ from *lawaᶜa* لَوَعَ "to suffer, burn" and *h(a)ārun* هَارٌ "undermined" used instead of *h(a)āʾirun* هَائرٌ underlyingly *h(a)āwirun* هَاوِرٌ from *hawara* هَوَرَ "to demolish". Hence these examples of active participles are formed according to the pattern *fālun* and not *fāᶜilun.* The phonological changes concerning one of these examples, e.g. *h(a)āwiᶜun* هَاوِعٌ that becomes *h(a)āᶜun* هَاعٌ "vomitting", are the following: *h(a)āwiᶜun* هَاوِعٌ with the 2nd radical *w* vowelled by a kasra and preceded by an *ā* becomes *h(a)āʾiᶜun* هائِعٌ after that the *wi* is changed into an *ʾi.* The procedure resulting in the elision of the 2nd weak radical is that the 2nd radical *w* vowelled by a kasra in *h(a)āwiᶜun* هَاوِعٌ is influenced by the fatḥa of the *h* preceding the *ā,* on account of the principle that the *ā* is not taken into account because of its vowellessness. So the *wi* is changed into an *ā* so that it becomes *h(a)āāᶜun* هَااعٌ. As there is in it a cluster of two vowelless alifs, one of them is elided so that it becomes *h(a)āᶜun* هَاعٌ.

**23- It is impossible to have a word beginning with a vowelless letter**

Ibn Ǧinnī, *Munṣif I,* 53) writes that the case of those who pretend that one can start with a vowelless letter is similar to the case of the sophists who doubt of evident things and of those whose mind is deficient. However, he notes in *Ḫaṣāʾiṣ I,* 91, that his teacher Abū ᶜAlī did not seem to express a dislike that the words in Persian can begin with a vowelless letter.

This is why for instance the imperfect prefix *t* of the 3rd person of the fem. sing., e.g. *taḍribu* تَضْرِبُ "she hits", is not rendered vowelless, i.e. *tḍribu* تْضْرِبُ, in the same manner as the suffixed *t* of feminization of the perfect does, e.g. *ḍarabat* ضَرَبَتْ "she hit", because of the principle that it is impossible to begin a word with a vowelless letter (cf. Åkesson, *Ibn Mas*$^c$*ūd,* the Commentary (102).

This rule implies that no phonological change can affect the initial segment of verbs with 1st weak radical. Hence, this means that the *w* in *wa*$^c$*ada* وَعَدَ "he promised" cannot be made vowelless resulting in *w*$^c$*ada* وْعَدَ, because of the impossibility of beginning the word with a vowelless segment (cf. ibid 270: fol. 25b-26a).

*23.1 The case of the connective hamza:*

According to a few grammarians, the connective prefixed hamza should by principle have been vowelless because it is a prefix, and it is prior to consider a prefix as being vowelless than vowelled (cf. Ibn al-Anbārī, Inṣāf Q. 107, 310). However, as it is impossible to begin a word with a vowelless consonant, Ibn Mas$^c$ūd (cf. Åkesson, *Ibn Mas*$^c$*ūd,* the Commentary (111)) remarks that the kasra is given to it, as by principle the kasra is given to the vowelless consonant. According to the Basrans the connective hamza is by principle given the kasra. The Kufans believe however that the connective hamza should follow in its vowel the vowel of the 2nd radical of the verb (for the debate see Ibn al-Anbārī, *Inṣāf* Q. 107, 309-312 and cf. Bohas, *Étude* 95-105).

*23.2 The prefixation of the prosthetic hamza to avoid beginning the word with a vowelless letter in the cases of the assimilation of the vowelled prefixed t of Form V tafa$^{cc}$ala or Form VI taf(a)ā$^{c}$ala to the 1st vowelled radical following it:*

The prefixed *t* of Form V and VI is assimilated to the 1st radical of the verb (cf. Zamaḫšarī, 196, Åkesson, *Ibn Mas$^{c}$ūd* 202: fol. 21a, de Sacy, I, 220-221, Wright, II, 64-65, $^{c}$Abd al-Tawwāb, *Taṭawwur* 29) and the prosthetic hamza vowelled by a kasra, the *$^{ɔ}$i,* is prefixed to the word in order to avoid beginning the word with a vowelless segment in the following cases:

1- the 1st radical is the *t,* e.g. Form V *tatarrasa* تَتَرَّسَ "shielded himself" that becomes after the assimilation *ttarasa* تَّرَسَ and the prosthetic hamza vowelled by a kasra, the *ʾi,* is prefixed to prevent beginning the word with a vowelless segment, resulting in *ʾittarasa* إتَّرَسَ.

2- the 1st radical is the interdental and surd *ṯ,* e.g. Form VI *taṯ(a)āqala* تَثَاقَلَ "to be borne down heavily" that becomes after the assimilation *ʾiṯṯ(a)āqala* إثَّاقَلَ (cf. Åkesson, *Ibn Masᶜūd* 202: fol. 21a, Howell, IV, fasc. II, 1829, Lane, I, 344, Penrice, *Dictionary* 25). The vowelled alveolar and surd *t* prefix vowelled by a fatḥa, the *ta,* is assimilated to the vowelled interdental and surd 1st radical *ṯ* vowelled by a fatḥa, the *ṯa,* resulting in *ṯṯāqala* ثَّاقَلَ and the prosthetic hamza vowelled by a kasra, the *ʾi,* is prefixed to prevent beginning the word with a vowelless segment, resulting in *ʾiṯṯ(a)āqala* إثَّاقَلَ.

3- the 1st radical is the alveolar and voiced *d,* e.g. Form VI *tad(a)āraʾa* تَدَارَأَ "to repel" that becomes after the assimilation *ʾidd(a)āraʾa* إدَّارَأَ (cf. Howell, IV, fasc. II, 1829, Lane, I, 865, Penrice, *Dictionary* 47). The vowelled alveolar and surd *t* prefix vowelled by a fatḥa, the *ta,* is assimilated to the vowelled alveolar and voiced 1st radical *d* vowelled by a fatḥa, the *da,* resulting in *dd(a)āra'a* دّارأ and the prosthetic hamza vowelled by a kasra, the *'i,* is prefixed to prevent beginning the word with a vowelless segment resulting in *'idd(a)āra'a* إدّارأ.

4- the 1st radical is the interdental and voiced *d̲,* e.g. Form VI *tad̲(a)ākara* تَذَاكَرَ "to be reminded" that becomes after the assimilation *'id̲d̲(a)ākara* إذّاكَرَ (cf. Howell, IV, fasc. II, 1829, Lane, I, 968, Penrice, *Dictionary* 52). The vowelled alveolar and surd *t* prefix, the *ta,* is assimilated to the vowelled interdental and voiced 1st radical *d̲a* resulting in *d̲d̲(a)ākara* ذّاكَرَ and the prosthetic hamza vowelled by a kasra, the *'i,* is prefixed to prevent beginning the word with a vowelless segment, resulting in *'id̲d̲(a)ākara* إذّاكَرَ.

5- the 1st radical is the dental, voiced and sibilant *z,* e.g. Form V *tazayyana* تَزَيَّنَ "to decorate itself" that becomes after the assimilation *'izzayyana* إزّيَّنَ (cf. Howell, IV, fasc. II, 1829, Lane, I, 1279, Wright, II, 64, Penrice, *Dictionary* 64). The alveolar and soft vowelled *t* prefix, the *ta,* is assimilated to the vowelled dental and sibilant 1st radical *z,* the *za,* resulting in *zzayyana* زَيَّنَ and the prosthetic hamza vowelled by a kasra, the *ᵓi,* is prefixed to prevent beginning the word with a vowelless segment, resulting in *ᵓizzayyana* إزَّيَّنَ.

6- the 1st radical is the dental, surd and sibilant *s,* e.g. Form V *tasammaᶜa* تَسَمَّعَ "to listen" that becomes after the assimilation *ᵓissammaᶜa* إسَّمَّعَ (cf. Howell, IV, fasc. II, 1829, Lane, I, 1427, 1428, Wright, II, 65, Penrice, *Dictionary* 72). The vowelled alveolar and soft *t* prefix, the *ta,* is assimilated to the vowelled dental and sibilant 1st radical *s,* the *sa,* resulting in *ssammaᶜa* سَّمَّعَ and the prosthetic hamza vowelled by a kasra, the *ᵓi,* is prefixed to prevent beginning the word with a vowelless segment, resulting in *ᵓissammaᶜa* إسَّمَّعَ.

7- the 1st radical is the pre-palatal and surd *š,* An example is Form VI *tašāǧara* تَشَاجَرَ "to be embroiled" that becomes after the assimilation *ᵓiššāǧara* إشَّاجَرَ (cf. Howell, IV, fasc. II, 1829). The vowelled alveolar and surd *t* prefix, the *ta,* is assimilated to the vowelled pre-palatal and surd 1st radical *š,* the *ša*, resulting in *sšāǧara* شَّاجَرَ and the prosthetic hamza vowelled by a kasra, the ʾi, is prefixed to prevent beginning the word with a vowelless segment, resulting in ʾiššāǧara إِشَّجَرَ.

8- the 1st radical is the dental, surd and sibilant ṣ, e.g. Form VI taṣ(a)ābara تَصَابَرَ "to bear patiently" that becomes after the assimilation ʾiṣṣ(a)ābara إِصَّابَرَ (cf. Howell, IV, fasc. II, 1829, Lane, II, 1643). The vowelled alveolar and surd t prefix, the ta, is assimilated to the vowelled dental and covered 1st radical ṣ, the ṣa, resulting in ṣṣ(a)ābara صَّابَرَ and the prosthetic hamza vowelled by a kasra, the ʾi, is prefixed to prevent beginning the word with a vowelless segment, resulting in ʾiṣṣ(a)ābara إِصَّابَرَ.

9- the 1st radical is the alveolar and voiced ḍ, e.g. Form VI taḍ(a)āraba تَضَارَبَ "to fight" that becomes after the assimilation ʾiḍḍ(a)āraba إِضَّارَبَ (cf. Howell, IV, fasc. II, 1829). The vowelled alveolar and surd t prefix, the ta, is assimilated to the alveolar and covered vowelled 1st radical ḍ, the ḍa, resulting in ḍḍ(a)āraba ضَّارَبَ and the prosthetic hamza vowelled by a kasra, the ʾi, is prefixed to prevent beginning the word with a vowelless segment, resulting in ʾiḍḍ(a)āraba إِضَّارَبَ.

10- the 1st radical is the alveolar and voiced *ṭ*, e.g. Form V *taṭahhara* تَطَهَّرَ "to purify one's-self" that becomes after the assimilation *ʾiṭṭahhara* إِطَّهَّرَ (cf. Åkesson, *Ibn Masᶜūd* 202: fol. 21a, Howell, IV, fasc. II, 1829, Lane, II, 1887, Penrice, *Dictionary* 91). The vowelled alveolar and surd *t* prefix, the *ta,* is assimilated to the vowelled alveolar and covered 1st radical *ṭ*, the *ṭa,* resulting in *ṭṭahhara* طَّهَّرَ and the prosthetic hamza vowelled by a kasra, the *ʾi,* is prefixed to prevent beginning the word with a vowelless segment, resulting in *ʾiṭṭahhara* إِطَّهَّرَ.

11- the 1st radical is the interdental and voiced *ẓ*, *e*.g. Form VI *taẓ(a)ālama* تَظَالَمَ "to wrong" that becomes after the assimilation *ʾiẓẓ(a)ālam* إِظَّالَمَ (cf. Howell, IV, fasc. II, 1829). The vowelled alveolar and surd *t* prefix, the *ta,* is assimilated to the vowelled interdental and covered 1st radical *ẓ*, the *ẓa,* resulting in *ẓẓ(a)ālama* ظَّالَمَ and the prosthetic hamza, the *ʾi,* is prefixed to prevent beginning the word with a vowelless segment, resulting in *ʾiẓẓ(a)ālama* إِظَّالَمَ.

## 24- Two vowelless letters cannot be combined together

*24.1 In verbs with 2nd weak radical:*

Examples in which the disliked combination of two vowelless letters is prevented to happen are in verbs with 2nd weak radical that occur in the 2nd and 3rd person of the fem. pl. of the imperfect in which the vowelled *–n,* the suffix *–na,* is suffixed to.

An example is the underlying forms *taḫ(a)āfna* تَخَافْنَ "you are afraid /fem. pl." and *yaḫ(a)āfna* يَخَافْنَ "they are afraid /fem. pl." - (and the 1st person is *ʾa-ḫ(a)āfu* أخَافُ "I am afraid" and the 2nd person of the masc. sing. is *taḫ(a)āfu* تَخَافُ "you are afraid") - from *ḫawafa* خَوَفَ, a verb with 2nd radical *w.* The 3rd radical becomes vowelless through the suffixation of the *-na,* which entails a cluster of two vowelless segments, the *ā* and the *f,* which is the reason why the *ā* is elided resulting in *taḫafna* تَخَفْنَ and *yaḫafna* يَخَفْنَ.

The same phonological changes occur with the underlying forms *tab(i)īᶜna* تَبِيعْنَ "you sell /fem. pl." and *yab(i)īᶜna* يَبِيعْنَ "they sell /fem. pl." - (and the 1st person is *ᵓab(i)īᶜu* أَبِيعُ "I sell" and the 2nd person of the masc. sing. is *tab(i)īᶜu* تَبِيعُ "you sell") - from *bayaᶜa* بَيَعَ, a verb with 2nd radical *y*. The *ī* is elided resulting in *tabiᶜna* تَبِعْنَ and *yabiᶜna* يَبِعْنَ.

*24.1.1 At the end of the word:*

*24.1.1.1 In the case of an imperfect, active, Energetic II which occurs before a vowelless letter in the 2nd word:*

The single *n* in a case of an imperfect, active, Energetic II is suppressed when a vowelless letter occurs after it in another word in order to avoid the cluster of two vowelless consonants.

This is noticed in *l(a)ā tuh(i)īna* لا تُهِينَ "do not humiliate" which occurs instead of *l(a)ā tuh(i)īnan* لا تُهِينَنْ that precedes a word starting with the definite article, namely *l-faq(i)īra* ٱلْفَقِيرَ "the poor" and thus implies a cluster of two vowelless consonants, in the following verse said by al-Aḍbaṭ b. Quraiᶜ al-

Sa^c^dī, cited by Zamaḫšarī, 156, Ibn Ya^c^īš, IX, 43, 44, Ibn ^c^Aqīl, II, 316, Alee, *Wasīṭ* 227 sq., Ibn Manẓūr, V, 3751, Howell, II-III, 442, 717, Daqr, *Mu^c^ǧam* 416, Åkesson, *Ibn Mas^c^ūd,* the Commentary (125 b):

" لا تُهِينَ الْفَقِيرَ عَلَّكَ تَرْكَعَ يَوْماً وَالدَّهْرُ قَدْ رَفَعَهُ".

*"Lā tuhīna l-faqīra ^c^allaka ^ɔ^an tar-*

*ka^c^a yawman wa-l-dahru qad rafa^c^ah".*

"Do not humiliate the poor: maybe that you may be low

one day,

when fortune has raised him".

*24.2 In weak 3rd radical verbs:*

Two examples can be analyzed. The first one is a verb with 3rd weak radical which has a suffix attached preceding the second word, e.g. *da^c^aw(u)ū l-qawma* دَعَوُا ٱلْقَوْمَ "they called for the people" originally *da^c^aw l-qawma* دَعَوْا ٱلْقَوْمَ and the second one is a verb with 2nd weak radical whose 3rd radical is given a vowel of juncture before the vowelless 1st letter of the article *–al* in the word following it, e.g. *quli l-ḥaqqa* قُلِ ٱلْحَقَّ "say /masc. sing. the truth" originally *qul l-ḥaqqa* قُلْ ٱلْحَقَّ.

In the first example, the verb *da<sup>c</sup>aw* دَعَوْا analyzed by itself, is a perfect occurring in the 3rd person of the masc. pl. It has the suffixed pronoun of the agent, the *w* of the pl., vowelless followed by the *alif mamdūda* when there is not a combination of two vowelless letters that occurs due to the second word. However, when it is followed by a noun to which the *-l* of the definite article following the *waṣla* is prefixed to, as in *da<sup>c</sup>aw(u)ū l-qawma* دَعَوُا ٱلْقَوْمَ, the suffixed pronoun of the agent, the *w,* is given ḍamma, which is a vowel of juncture, to avoid the cluster of two vowelless letters, namely the vowelless *w* that is the pronoun of the agent in دَعَوْا and the vowelless *l-* following the *waṣla* of the definite article prefixed to the second word *l-qawma, i.e.* دَعَوُا ٱلْقَوْمَ (cf. Åkesson, *Ibn Mas<sup>c</sup>ūd* 284: fol. 28a).

In the second example, *quli l-ḥaqqa* قُلِ ٱلْحَقَّ "say /masc. sing. the truth", the *w* is at first elided in the imperative *qul* "say /masc.

sing." that is used instead of *q(u)ūl* قُولْ to avoid the cluster of two vowelless letters, the *w* and the *l*.

The general principle that is adapted to avoid a cluster of two vowelless letters that occurs in two words is that the 1st vowelless letter, which is the ultimate letter of the first word, is vowelled by a kasra, which is a vowel of juncture.

In the example *quli l-ḥaqqa* قُلِ ٱلْحَقَّ, the 3rd radical *l* of *qul* قُلْ, which is originally vowelless as it marks the imperative, is given a kasra, i.e. *quli* قُلِ to avoid the cluster of two sukūns, its own sukūn of the imperative and the sukūn of the *-l* of the article *-al,* prefixed to the word that occurs after it, i.e. *l-ḥaqqa* ٱلْحَقَّ (cf. ibid, the Commentary (288)).

In more anomalous cases, the vowel of juncture can be a ḍamma. This occurs for the purpose of alleviation when the letter that precedes it or follows it is vowelled by a ḍamma.

Examples in which the ḍamma precedes it are: *qulu ḍrib* قُلُ ٱضرِبْ "say strike! /masc. sing.", sur. 73: 2 *(qumu l-layla)* قُمُ ٱللَّيْلَ "Stand (to prayer) by night" in the reading of some instead of *qumi l-layla* قُمِ ٱللَّيْلَ (for a study see Howell, IV, fasc. I, 1024 sqq.) and the sur. 10: 101 *(qulu nẓurū)* قُلُ ٱنْظُرُوا "Say: Behold /masc. pl)" (cf. Sībawaihi, II, 299). An example in which the ḍamma occurs in the word following it is: the sur. 12: 31 *(wa-q(a)ālatu ḫruǧ)* وَقَالَتُ ٱخْرُجْ "And she said (to Joseph), "Come out before them" (cf. Sībawaihi, II, 299), in which the vowel of juncture, the ḍamma, of the *t* in *q(a)ālatu* قَالَتُ is made to agree with ḍamma of the *r* in *ḫruǧ* ٱخْرُجْ.

*24.3 Cases in which the combination of two vowelless letters can occur:*

Examples are nouns beginning with a conjunctive hamza vowelled by a fatḥa to which the interrogative hamza, the *ʾa,* is prefixed to, e.g. *ʾaʾaymunu* أَأَيْمُنُ that results in *ʾ(a)āymunu* (with madda over the alif) آيْمُنُ in the example *ʾ(a)āymunu l-lāhi yam(i)īnuka* آيْمُنُ اللّه يَمينُكَ originally *ʾaʾaymunu l-lāhi yam(i)īnuka* أَأَيْمُنُ اللّه يَمينُكَ "Is the blessing of God your oath?", and nouns in which the definite article *ʾal* is prefixed to, as e.g. *ʾaʾal-Ḥasanu* أَأَلْحَسنُ that results in *ʾ(a)āl-Ḥasanu* (with *madda* over the alif) آلْحَسنُ in the example *ʾāl-Ḥasanu ʿindaka* آلْحَسنُ

عنْدَكَ originally *ʾaʾal-Ḥasanu ᶜindaka* أألْحَسنُ عنْدَكَ "Is al-Ḥasan by you?" (cf. Howell, IV, fasc. I, 1003, Åkesson, *Ibn Masᶜūd,* Commentary (229)).

The cluster of two vowelless letters is also accepted in the following cases (cf. Howell, IV, fasc. I, 988 sqq.):

1- in a word occurring in pause.

2- in a word in which an assimilated letter is preceded by a weak letter, e.g. *ḫuwayṣṣatun* "dear particular friend" in which both the *y* and the 1st *ṣ* among the doubled ṣāds is vowelless.

3- in uniflected nouns such as *ᶜayn* عَيْنْ, *q(a)āf* قَافْ and *Bakr* بَكْرْ "Bakr".

4- when the numerals are enumerated, e.g. *ʾiṯn(a)ān* إثْنَانْ "two".

5- in such an expression as *l(a)āh(a)ā l-l(a)āh* لاهَا ألله in the oath, in which both the final *ā* of *l(a)āh(a)ā* لاهَا and the *l-* of the definite article of *l-lāh* ألله are vowelless.

## 25- Two identical letters of which the 1st is vowelless and the 2nd vowelled are assimilated

*25.1 In one word:*

An example of such a case is *maddun* مَدٌّ "an extension" originally مَدْدٌ that is formed according to the pattern *faᶜlun* فَعْلٌ, in which the necessary assimilation of the 1st *d* to the 2nd *d* is carried out.

Another example is Form VIII *ᵓittağara* إتَّجَرَ "to trade" originally إتْتَجَرَ (cf. Åkesson, *Ibn Masᶜūd* 196: fol. 19a) from *tağara* تَجَرَ with 1st *t* radical. In the base form *ᵓittağara* إتْتَجَرَ, the 1st vowelless *t* radical is followed by the vowelled *t* infix, the *ta,* of Form VIII *ᵓiftaᶜala* إِفْتَعَلَ, which necessitates the assimilation of the *t* to the *t*. Hence *ᵓittağara* إتَّجَرَ is written with one *t* carrying the *šadda* in Arabic as an indication of the assimilation.

*25.2 In two words:*

The assimilation can be carried out from a 1st vowelless letter, which is the last letter of a word, to a 2nd identical vowelled letter that is the initial segment of the word following it.

An example of such a case is *ʾiḫšaw w(a)āqidan* إخْشَوْ وَاقِداً "Fear [2nd person of the masc. pl. of the imperative] one who sets fire!" (cf. Sībawaihi, II, 457) in which the 1st *w* is vowelless and the 2nd *w* is vowelled by a fatḥa. The example becomes after the assimilation of the vowelless *w* to the vowelled *wa, ʾiḫšaw w(a)āqidan* إخْشَوَّاقِداً with the 2nd *w* carrying the *šadda* as an indication of the assimilation.

**26- Two identical letters which are both vowelled are usually assimilated except in some cases**

<u>*26.1 In one word:*</u>

The combination of two identical vowelled segments leads mostly to the assimilation, except in some anomalous cases as in the case of *ḥayiya* حَيِيَ "to live", in the coordinatives and in somes measures that can be mixed up with other measures.

The assimilation occurs:

1- In examples of doubled verbs in the perfect, e.g. *sarara* سَرَرَ resulting after the assimilation in *sarra* سَرَّ.

2- In examples of verbs of Form V *tafa*ᶜᶜ*ala* تَفَعَّلَ or Form VI *taf(a)ā*ᶜ*ala* تَفَاعَلَ in which the vowelled prefixed *t* is assimilated to the 1st vowelled radical *t* following it. An example is Form V *tatarrasa* تَتَرَّسَ "shielded himself" that becomes after the assimilation ᵓ*ittarasa* إتَّرَسَ (cf. Howell, IV, fasc. II, 1829). The vowelled *t* prefix, i.e. the *ta,* is assimilated to the vowelled 1st radical *t,* i.e. the *ta,* resulting in *ttarasa* تَّرَسَ and the prosthetic hamza, the ᵓ*i,* is then prefixed to prevent beginning the word with a vowelless segment.

3- In examples of verbs of Form VIII in the imperfect *yafta*ᶜ*ilu* يَفْتَعِلُ in which the vowelled infixed *t* is assimilated to the 2nd vowelled radical *t* following it. An example is *yaqtatilu* يَقْتَتِلُ "to contend among themselves" that becomes after the assimilation *yaqattilu* يَقَتِّلُ (cf. Åkesson, *Ibn Mas*ᶜ*ūd* 200: fol. 20b). The vowelled *t* prefix, i.e. the *ta,* is assimilated to the vowelled 2nd radical, i.e. *ti,* after that its fatḥa vowel is shifted to the 1st radical *q*. It can be noted that both variants *yaqattilu* يَقَتِّلُ and *yaqittilu* يِقِتِّلُ occur (cf. Zamaḫšarī, 195, Howell, IV, fasc. II, 1807).

*26.2 The assimilation does not occur:*

*26.2.1 The anomalous case of ḥayiya* حَيِيَ:

The assimilation is not carried out in some dialectal variants in the doubled verb with two weak radicals *ḥayiya* حَيِيَ "to live" (for discussions concerning it see Sībawaihi, II, 430-431, Zamaḫšarī, 187, Ibn ᶜAqīl, II, 588, Åkesson, *Ibn Masᶜūd* 194: fol. 18a, Howell, IV, fasc. I, 1624 sqq., fasc. II, 1693 sqq., Wright, II, 94-95, Vernier, I, 342-343, de Sacy, I, 259-260). In spite of the fact that two vowelled identical segments are combined in it, namely the *yi* and the *ya,* they are not in most cases assimilated together resulting in *ḥayya* حَيَّ. The assimilation is carried out however in some dialectal variants. The reason why some prefer not to assimilate the yāᵓs in the perfect resulting in *ḥayya* حَيَّ, is that they feel obliged by analogy to assimilate them in the imperfect causing the ḍamma to vowel the *y* which is deemed as a heavy combination, i.e. *yaḥayyu* would have to be said instead of *yaḥy(a)ā* يَحْيَى with final *ᵓalif maqṣūra.* Those who assimilate in the perfect by saying *ḥayya* حَيَّ consider both yāᵓs as two identical vowelled segments in one word. They avoid however to assimilate in the imperfect because of the implied heavy combination. This means that *yaḥy(a)ā* يَحْيَى with final *alif maqṣūra* occurs by all instead of *yaḥayyu* يَحَيُّ. Furthermore, the 3rd radical *y* has been dropped by some in the perfect of the 3rd person of the masc. pl., who use *ḥay(u)ū* حَيُوا instead of *ḥayiy(u)ū* حَيِيُوا (cf. Sībawaihi, II, 431, Ibn Manẓūr, II, 1080). This elision of the *y* implies that it is considered as unnecessary to the word's structure (cf. Åkesson, *Ibn Mas$^c$ūd* 194: fol. 18a). In the light that the 2nd letter among two identical letters is not necessary for the structure of the word, it can be understood why the assimilation is not always carried out in the perfect *ḥayiya* حَيِيَ, as the condition of the assimilation is that the 2nd letter among the identical letters should be existent in the structure and not submitted to an elision.

*26.2.2 In the coordinatives and in some special measures:*

The assimilation is forbidden in *al-ʾilḥāqīyāt* الإلحاقيات "the co-ordinatives", in spite of the vowelling of two identical segments in them. These patterns refer to those words that are rendered quasi-coordinate to other words of which the radicals are greater in number than theirs (cf. Lane, II 3008). An example is *qardadun* قَرْدَدٌ "elevated ground" (cf. Sībawaihi, II, 448, Åkesson, *Ibn Mas*$^{c}$*ūd* 194: 17b) from the root *qarida* قَرِدَ "it became contracted together", in which the 2nd *d* is added to the form, and no assimilation is to be carried out from the first vowelled *d,* the *da,* to the other vowelled *d,* the *dun,* on account that the word is quasi-coordinate to the measure *fa*$^{c}$*lalun* فَعْلَلٌ (cf. Lane, II, 2513).

The assimilation is as well forbidden in some words that are formed according to special measures (cf. Sībawaihi, II, 445-446, Åkesson, *Ibn Mas*$^{c}$*ūd* 194: fol. 18a) as *fa*$^{c}$*ilun* فَعِلٌ, *fu*$^{c}$*ulun* فُعُلٌ, *fu*$^{c}$*alun* فُعَلٌ and *fa*$^{c}$*alun* فَعَلٌ, so that they are not mixed up with other words in which the assimilation is carried out. Some examples are:

- *ṣakikun* صَكِكٌ "the colliding of the knees in running" formed according to *fa$^c$ilun* فَعِلٌ to avoid mixing it up with *ṣakkun* صَكٌّ "a written acknowledgement of a debt".

- *sururun* سُرُرٌ "bedsteads" formed according to *fu$^c$ulun* فُعُلٌ to avoid mixing it up with *surrun* سُرٌّ "the navel- string of a child".

- *ǧudadun* جُدَدٌ "the stripes that are on the back of the ass" formed according to *fu$^c$alun* فُعَلٌ to avoid mixing it up with *ǧuddun* جُدٌّ "a part of the river near the land".

- *ṭalalun* طَلَلٌ "the remains of a dwelling or house" formed according to *fa$^c$alun* فَعَلٌ to avoid mixing it up with *ṭallun* طَلٌّ "weak rain".

## 27- The vowelless *w* preceded by a fatḥa is changed into an *ā*

*27.1 In verbs with 2nd w radical:*

An example is a verb that is formed according to the conjugation *yaf$^c$alu,* e.g. *yaẖwafu* يَخْوَفُ "he is afraid". The phonological change involves two steps: the first is the transfer of the *w's* fatḥa to the vowelless 1st radical *ḫ* preceding it, which results in *yaḫawfum* يَخَوْفُ, and the second one is the change of the vowelless *w* into an *ā* on account of the influence of the fatḥa preceding it, which results in *yaḫ(a)āfu* يَخَافُ. These two steps answer to two different principles: the first is that when the glide is vowelled and follows a sukūn its vowel is shifted to the vowelless segment preceding it and the second is that when the glide is vowelless and preceded by a fatḥa it is changed into an *ā*.

**28- The vowelless *w* preceded by a kasra is changed into a *y***

*28.1 In verbs with 1st w radical:*

An example is an imperative that is formed according to *ʾifʿal,* e.g. *ʾiwǧal* إِوْجَلْ "dread!" in which the *w* is vowelless and preceded by the kasra of the connective hamza. The phonological change is that the *w* is changed into a *y,* namely *ʾiyǧal* إِيجَلْ on account of the influence of the kasra (cf. Wright, II, 80).

Another example is *ʾifʿil,* e.g. *ʾiwʿid* إِوْعِدْ "promise /masc sing.". The phonological procedures are that the vowelless *w* is at first changed into a *y* on account of the kasra preceding it, namely *ᵓiyᶜid* إِيعْدْ (cf. Wright, II, 78, de Sacy, I, 238), then both the hamza vowelled by a kasra, namely the *ᵓi,* and the *y* are elided resulting in *ᶜid.* This elision of the 1st radical *w* changed into *y* seems to be on the analogy of its elision in the imperfect *taᶜidu* تَعِدُ.

In the Form VIII of the perfect *ᵓiftaᶜala* إِفْتَعَلَ, e.g. *ᵓiwtaᶜada* إِوْتَعَدَ "to accept a promise", the *w* is changed into a *y* on account of the kasra of the connective hamza preceding it, namely *ᵓiytaᶜada* إِيتَعَدَ, and the *y* is assimilated to the infixed *t,* resulting in *ᵓittaᶜada* إِتَّعَدَ.

**29- The vowelless *w* preceding a vowelled *y* is changed into a *y* and both yāᵓs are assimilated**

*29.1 In verbs with 2nd weak radical:*

An example is *mawyitun* مَوْيِتٌ "a dead man", in which the *y* vowelled by a kasra is preceded by the vowelless 2nd radical *w.* The phonological change is carried out by the change of the *w* into a *y* and the assimilation of the *y* to the *y*. Thus *mawyitun* مَوْيِتٌ becomes *mayyitun* مَيِّتٌ after that the *w* is changed into a *y* and the yā'ʾs are assimilated (cf, Åkesson, *Ibn Masʿūd.* the Commentary, (264)).

Another example is *sayyidun* سَيِّدٌ "a lord", which is originally *saywidun* سَيْوِدٌ in which the *w* is changed into a y, i.e. *sayyidun* سَيْيِدٌ, and both yāʾs are assimilated, i.e. *sayyidun* سَيِّدٌ (cf. Hindāwī, *Manāhiğ* 357).

**30- The vowelless *w* following a y and preceding a kasra is elided**

<u>*30.1 In verbs with 1st w radical:*</u>

An example is Form I of the verb with 1st *w* radical *yawʿidu* يَوْعِدُ "he promises" in which the *w* follows the imperfect prefix *y* and precedes a kasra resulting in a disliked combination, which is why it is elided, i.e. *yaʿidu* يَعِدُ.

**31- The vowelless *y* preceded by a ḍamma is changed into a *w***

*31.1 In verbs with 1st y radical:*

An example is an imperfect of the passive voice of Form I *yufᶜalu* يُفْعَلُ, e.g. *yuysaru* يُيْسَرُ that becomes *yuwsaru* يُوْسَرُ > *y(u)ūsaru* يُوسَرُ "is pleased".

The same change of the *y* into *w* is carried out in the active voice of Form IV of the imperfect *yuysiru* يُيْسِرُ that becomes *yuwsiru* يُوْسِرُ > *y(u)ūsiru* يُوسِرُ "is well off" (cf. Wright, II, 50). Thus *yuysiru* يُيْسِرُ with the vowelless *y* preceded by a ḍamma becomes *yuwsiru* يُوْسِرُ with the *y* changed into a *w*. As it has its vowelless *w* preceded by a ḍamma, it becomes *y(u)ūsiru* يُوسِرُ with the *w* changed into an *ū*.

The same applies for the active participle Form IV *muysirun* مُيْسِرٌ that becomes *muwsirun* مُوْسِرٌ > *m(u)ūsirun* مُوسِرٌ "is prosperous" (cf. Åkesson, *Ibn Masᶜūd* 286: fol. 28a-28b). Thus *muysirun* مُيْسِرٌ with the vowelless 1st radical *y* preceded by a ḍamma becomes *muwsirun* مُوْسِرٌ with the *y* changed into a *w*.

As *muwsirun* مُوْسِرٌ has its vowelless *w* preceded by a ḍamma it becomes *m(u)ūsirun* مُوسِرٌ with the *w* changed into an *ū*. The reason of the change of the vowelless *y* into a *w* is the influence of the ḍamma of the segment preceding the *y* and the faintness of the nature of the vowelless segment in relation to the vowelled segment (cf. Åkesson, *Ibn Masʿūd* 286: fol. 28b).

**32- The *w* or *y* that is vowelled by a fatḥa and preceded by a fatḥa is changed into an *ā* except in a few cases**

*32.1 In verbs:*

This combination occurs in verbs with 2nd or 3rd weak radical and in nouns and adjectives. The *w* or *y* is changed into an *ā* in verbs with 2nd weak radical and in nouns and adjectives, and into an *ā* or *alif mamdūda* in verbs with 3rd radical *w* or into an *alif maqṣūra* in verbs with 3rd radical *y*. The *w* or *y* remains sound in some specific cases.

The cases that can be mentioned are the perfects of verbs with 2nd or 3rd weak radical in the 3rd person of the masc. sing.

An example of a verb with weak 2nd radical *w* is *qawala* قَوَلَ > *q(a)āla* قَالَ "to say".

An example of a verb with weak 2nd radical *y* is *baya*$^c$*a* بَيَعَ > *b(a)ā*$^c$*a* بَاعَ "to sell".

In the case of verbs with 3rd weak radical *w,* the *w* is changed into an *alif mamdūda,* e.g. *ġazawa* غَزَوَ > *ġaz(a)ā* غَزَا "to raid" and in the case of verbs with 3rd weak radical *y,* the *y* is changed into an *alif maqṣūra,* e.g. *ramaya* رَمَيَ > *ram(a)ā* رَمَى "to throw".

*32.2 In nouns or adjectives:*

The phonological change is carried out in the noun or adjective on the condition that the noun is formed according to the verbal form *fa*$^c$*al* فَعَل. An example is *dawarun* دَوَرٌ with the 2nd radical *w* vowelled by a fatḥa and preceded by one that becomes *d(a)ārun* دَارٌ "house" after that the *wa* is changed into an *ā.* The phonological change that is carried out in this noun is not only due to the fact that its glide is vowelled by a fatḥa and is preceded by one, but also because it answers the condition of resembling the verbal form *fa<sup>c</sup>al* فَعَل (for this condition see Åkesson, *Ibn Mas<sup>c</sup>ūd* 284: fol. 27b, Bohas/Kouloughli, *Linguistic* 86). Thus no phonological change is carried out in nouns that lose their resemblance to a verbal form through the suffixation of a noun suffix.

**33- The *w* or *y* that is vowelled by a fatḥa and preceded by one is sound in these cases**

*33.1 In verbs:*

*33.1.1 To avoid the forbidden combination of two phonological changes:*

An example that can introduce a combination of two phonological changes, which is forbidden, is the doubly weak verb *ṭawaya* طَوَيَ in which the sequence *ya* preceded by a fatḥa is changed into an *(a)ā,* namely *ṭaw(a)ā* طَوَى [with final *alif maqṣūra]* "to fold" (cf. Åkesson, *Ibn Mas<sup>c</sup>ūd* 284: fol. 28a). It is not allowed after this change to change the sequence *wa* of *ṭaw(a)ā* preceded by a fatḥa into *(a)ā* that would result in *ṭ(a)āā*

طَاى as this would necessarily imply a cluster of two vowelless glides, the alifs: the *alif mamdūda* and the *alif maqṣūra,* which is forbidden.

*33.1.2 If the fatḥa preceding the w or y is ruled by the sukūn of another form:*

A factor that can hinder the change of the *w* or *y* that is vowelled by a fatḥa and preceded by one into an *ā,* is that the fatḥa of the letter preceding it in a specific form can be influenced theoretically by the sukūn of another form which it resembles in meaning, and thus this fatḥa is counted as ruled by a sukūn (cf. ibid, 284: fol. 27b-28a).

This is the case of some verbs of Form VIII *ʾiftaʿala* إِفْتَعَلَ with 2nd radical *w,* that have the meaning of Form VI *taf(a)āʿala* تَفَاعَلَ denoting the reciprocity, in which the *w* is counted as sound in them (cf. Sībawaihi, II, 399-401, Ibn Ǧinnī, *Ḫaṣāʾiṣ I.* 145-148, Zamaḫšarī, 180, Ibn Yaʿīš, X, 74-75, Howell, II-III, 275, IV, fasc. I, 1242-1243), and thus the sequence *awa* in them is not changed into *(a)ā.* Some examples are Form VIII *ʾiǧtawar(u)ū* إِجْتَوَرُوا "they became mutual neighbours" that did not become *ᵓiğt(a)ār(u)ū* إجْتَارُوا because it has the meaning of Form VI *tağ(a)āwar(u)ū* تَجَاوَرُوا. It is as though, in the case of Form VIII *ᵓiğtawara,* that the fatḥa preceding the *w* is counted as being ruled by the sukūn of the vowelless *ā* preceding the *w* in Form VI *tağ(a)āwara* تَجَاوَرَ (cf. Åkesson, *Ibn Masᶜūd* 284: fol. 28a), which is the reason why the *wa* is retained and the form did not become *ᵓiğt(a)āra* إجْتَارَ. So *ᵓiğtawara* إجْتَوَرَ is associated to *tağ(a)āwara* تَجَاوَرَ on account of its similarity of meaning to it, and in *tağ(a)āwara* تَجَاوَرَ, the vowelless *ā* prevented the change of the sequence *wa* into *(a)ā.* It is then as if the vowelless *ā* of *tağ(a)āwara* تَجَاوَرَ rules as well the *w* of *ᵓiğtawara* إجْتَوَرَ, in which the fatḥa becomes counted as a sukūn, and thus hinders any change to be carried out.

Another example is Form VIII *ᵓizdawağ(u)ū* إزْدَوَجُوا "they intermarried" that did not become *ᵓizd(a)āğ(u)ū* إزْداجُوا because it has the meaning of Form VI *taz(a)āwağ(u)ū* تَزَاوَجُوا.

The change of the sequence *awa* into *(a)ā* is necessary otherwise, e.g. *ʾiḫtawana* إِخْتَوَنَ that has the meaning of Form I *ḫ(a)āna* خَانَ, which becomes *ʾiḫt(a)āna* إِخْتَانَ "was unfaithful".

<u>*33.2 In nouns or adjectives:*</u>

<u>*33.2.1 If the noun or adjective is not formed according to faᶜal:*</u>

This occurs if the noun or adjective is not formed according to the verbal form *faᶜal* through the sufixation of the *tāʾ marbūṭa* or the *alif maqṣūra*.

Some examples are *ḥawakatun* حَوَكَةٌ "weavers", which is the pl. of *ḥ(a)āʾikun* حَائِكٌ and *ḫawanatun* خَوَنَةٌ "traitors", which is the pl. of *ḫ(a)āʾinun* خَائِنٌ (cf. Zamaḫšarī, 181, Åkesson, *Ibn Masᶜūd* 284: fol. 28a, Howell, IV, fasc. I, 1510). Both these triliterals differ from their verbs' measures *ḥawaka* حَوَكَ "to weave" and *ḫawana* خَوَنَ "to betray" through the *tāʾ marbūṭa* of feminization. This is the reason why the sequence *wa* is not changed into *(a)ā* in them, and serves through its retaining to give indication of their base forms.

An example of a noun to which the *alif maqṣūra* is suffixed to is *Ṣawar(a)ā* صَوَرَى "Ṣawar(a)ā, name of a water" (cf. Åkesson, *Ibn Mas*<sup></sup>*ūd* 284: fol. 28a), which is referred to as being the name of a water in Medīna (cf. Ibn Wallād, *Maqṣūr* 74). The sequence *wa* in it is retained and not changed into an *ā*. An example of an adjective is *ḥayad(a)ā* حَيَدَى "(a he-ass) shying at his own shadow because of his liveliness" (cf. Åkesson, *Ibn Mas*ᶜ*ūd* 284: fol. 28a, Howell, IV, fasc. I, 1251), that is formed according to the pattern *fa*ᶜ*al(a)ā* فَعَلَى, in which the *ya* is retained.

<u>*33.2.2 If the noun is meant to give clues to the base form:*</u>

An example of a noun in which the *w* is intended to notify of the base form is *qawadun* قَوَدٌ "retaliation" that refers to the root *q w d,* and of a noun in which the *y* is intended to notify of the base form is *ṣayadun* صَيَدٌ "a disease in a camel's head" (cf. Zamaḫšarī, 173, Åkesson, *Ibn Mas*ᶜ*ūd* 284: fol. 28a, Howell, IV, fasc. I, 1251) that refers to *s y d.* The sequence *wa* in *qawadun* قَوَدٌ is not changed into *(a)ā,* i.e. *qa(ā)dun* قَادٌ, in spite of its being vowelled with a fatḥa and preceded by one, as this would cause a confusion on whether the form is from the root *qawada* قَوَدَ "to lead" with the *w* as 2nd radical or the root *qayada* قَيَدَ "to bind" with the *y* as 2nd radical. The same goes for the *ya* in *ṣayadun* صَيَدٌ that is not changed into *(a)ā,* i.e. *ṣa(ā)dun* صَادٌ*,* as this would cause a confusion on whether the form is from the root *ṣawada* صَوَدَ with the *w* as 2nd radical, that is the base form of *al-ṣ(a)ādu* الصَّادُ "the [letter] ṣād" or the root *ṣayada* صَيَدَ "to hunt" with the *y* as 2nd radical.

### *33.2.3 If the noun refers in its meaning to intensive mobility:*

This is the case of the noun *ḥayaw(a)ānun* حَيَوَانٌ "animal, much life" (cf. Åkesson, *Ibn Masᶜūd* 284: fol. 28a, Howell, IV, fasc. I, 1409) in which no phonological change is carried out so that the word corresponds in mobility to what it represents, which is a mobile animal. It occurs in the sur. 29: 64 *(la-hya l-ḥayawānu)* لَهِيَ الْحَيَوَانُ "that is Life indeed". The variant *mawt(a)ānun* مَوْتَانٌ is its opposite in meaning, and on this account it is formed according to its pattern (cf. Ibn Manẓūr, VI,

4296, Åkesson, *Ibn Mas$^{c}$ūd* 284: fol. 28a, Lane, I, 679, 682, Howell, IV, fasc. I, 1244, 1409, 1465).

**34- The ḍamma vowelling the *w* is disliked**

Examples are found in verbs with 2nd radical *w* of the conjugation *yaf$^{c}$ulu* يَفْعُلُ that occur in the imperfect, e.g. *yaqwulu* يَقْوُلُ "he says" in which the *w* is vowelled by a ḍamma. What occurs is that the ḍamma is transferred to the *q* and then the *u* is assimilated to the *w* resulting in the long *ū,* i.e. *yaquwlu* يَقُوْلُ > *yaq(u)ūlu* يَقُولُ.

In the imperative, e.g. *ˀuqwul* "say!" أُقْوُلْ > *ˀuquwl* أُقُوْلْ > *uq(u)ūl* أُقُولْ, and then after the elision of the connective hamza and the *ū* > *qul* قُلْ and in the passive participle *maqwuwlun* > *maqw(u)ūlun* مَقْوُولٌ "what is said" > *maq(u)ūlun* مَقُولٌ.

It can be remarked that *maqwuwlun* > *maqw(u)ūlun* مَقْوُولٌ is conformable to the passive participle form *maf$^{c}$uwlun* / *maf$^{c}$(u)ūlun* مَفْعُولٌ.

Both the Banū Tamīm and the Ḥiğāzīs agree however upon making defective the passive participle with 2nd weak radical *w,* except for some forms that occur anomalously, e.g. *lafẓun maqw(u)ūlun* لَفْظٌ مَقْوُولٌ "a word said" and *ṯawbun maṣw(u)ūnun* ثَوْبٌ مَصْوُونٌ "a garment preserved", but the more used forms are *maq(u)ūlun* مَقُولٌ and *maṣ(u)ūnun* مَصُونٌ (for a study see Ibn Yaᶜīš, X, 80-81, Ibn ᶜAqīl, II, 575-576, Suyūṭī, *Muẓhir I,* 137, Howell, IV, fasc. I, 1505).

## 35- The ḍamma vowelling the *w* and preceded by a ḍamma is disliked

<u>*35.1 At the end of the word:*</u>

If the weak letter is a *w* vowelled by a ḍamma and preceded by a ḍamma, namely *–uwu,* occurring at the end of a word, it becomes *-uw* > *-(u)ū* after that the ḍamma is elided and the *w* is changed into an *ū:* lengthened *ū.*

An example of such a sequence is found in the verb with 3rd radical *w* in the imperfect of the 3rd person of the masc. sing. *yaġzuwu* يَغْزُوُ "he attacks" that becomes *yaġzuw* يَغْزُوْ / *yaġz(u)ū* يَغْزُو.

Likewise in the 3rd person of the masc. pl. *yaġzuw(u)ūna* يَغْزُوُونَ "they raid /masc. pl", the *w* is preceded by a ḍamma and followed by one. The phonological changes involve the elision of the *w's* ḍamma and the elision of the *w* on account of the occurrence of two vowelless letters: *the w* and the *ū.*

Hence: *yaġzuw(u)ūna* يَغْزُوُونَ > *yaġzuwūna* يَغْزُوون > *yaġz(u)ūna* يَغْزُون.

**36- The ḍamma vowelling the *y* and preceded by a kasra is disliked**

<u>*36.1 At the end of the word:*</u>

If the weak letter is a *y* vowelled by a ḍamma and preceded by a kasra, namely *–iyu,* occurring at the end of a word, it becomes *-iy* > *-(i)ī* after that the ḍamma is elided and the *y* is changed into an *ī:* lengthened *ī.*

An example of such a sequence is found in the verb with 3rd radical *y* in the imperfect of the 3rd person of the masc. sing. *yarmiyu* يَرْمِيُ "he throws" that becomes *yarmiy* > *yarm(i)ī* يَرْمِي.

**37- The kasra vowelling the *y* and preceded by a kasra is disliked**

An example in which such a sequence occurs is the verb with 3rd radical *y* in the imperfect of the 2nd person of the fem. sing. *tarmiy(i)īna* تَرْمِيِينَ that becomes *tarm(i)īna* تَرْمِينَ "you throw". The phonological changes involve the elision of the *y's* kasra and the elision of the *y* on account of the occurrence of two vowelless letters: *the y* and the *ī.*

Hence: *tarmiy(i)īna* تَرْمِيِينَ > *tarmiyīna* تَرْمِيْينَ > *tarm(i)īna* تَرْمِينَ.

**38- The ḍamma vowelling the *y* is disliked**

*38.1 In the middle of the word:*

*38.1.1 In the verb with 2nd y radical:*

The conjugation *faᶜula* فَعُلَ does not exit in the verb with 2nd radical *y* due to the dislike of having the 2nd radical *y* vowelled by a ḍamma (cf. Ibn Ǧinnī, *Munṣif I,* 244, Hindāwī, *Manāhiǧ* 354).

The common conjugations of this class can be grouped into the following:

1- *fa$^{c}$ala yaf$^{c}$ilu,* e.g. *baya$^{c}$a yabyi$^{c}$u* بَيَعَ يَبْيِعُ that becomes after the phonological change *bā$^{c}$a yabī$^{c}$u* بَاعَ يَبِيعُ "to sell".

2- *fa$^{c}$ila yaf$^{c}$alu,* e.g. *hayiba yahyabu* هَيِبَ يَهْيَبُ that becomes after the phonological change *hāba yahābu* هَابَ يَهَابُ "to fear".

<u>*38.1.2 In the passive participle of a verb with 2nd radical y:*</u>

An example is *maby(u)ū$^{c}$un* مَبْيُوعٌ "sold" in which the *y* is vowelled by a ḍamma. The 1st step of the phonological procedure that is carried out in it is the following (cf. Åkesson, *Ibn Mas$^{c}$ūd* 292: fol. 31a): *maby(u)w$^{c}$un* > *maby(u)ū$^{c}$un* مَبْيُوعٌ with the 2nd radical *y* vowelled by a ḍamma and preceded by a sukūn becomes *mabuyw$^{c}$un* مَبُيْوْعٌ and then *mabuyū$^{c}$un* مَبُيْوْعٌ after that the *y's* ḍamma is shifted to the *b* causing an occurrence of two vowelless segments: the *y* and the *ū*.

As with the passive participle with 2nd radical *w* *maqw(u)ūlun* مَقْوُولٌ (cf. par. 20), both Sībawaihi's and al-Aḫfaše's differences of opinions concerning the phonological changes that are carried out from *mabuyū*ᶜ*un* مَبْيُوعٌ to the result *mab(i)ī*ᶜ*un* مَبِيعٌ are applied (for discussions see Zamaḫšarī, 180-181, Ibn Yaᶜīš, X, 78-81, Åkesson, *Ibn Mas*ᶜ*ūd* 292: fols. 31a-31b, Howell, IV, fasc. I, 1498-1501). They can be illustrated as follows:

According to Sībawaihi, *mabuyū*ᶜ*un* مَبْيُوعٌ that has a cluster of a vowelless *y* and *ū* becomes *mabuy*ᶜ*un* مَبُيْعٌ after the elision of the infixed *ū*. As there is in it a vowelless *y* preceded by a ḍamma, the ḍamma is changed into a kasra so that it becomes *mabiy*ᶜ*un* مَبِيْعٌ. So according to his theory, *mabiy*ᶜ*un* مَبِيْعٌ is formed according to *mafi*ᶜ*lun* مَفِعْلٌ. It can be observed that in *mabiy*ᶜ*un* مَبِيْعٌ, the vowelless *y* is preceded by a kasra, which is the reason why the *y* is changed into an *ī*, namely *mab(i)ī*ᶜ*un* مَبِيعٌ.

According to al-Aḫfaš, *mabuyū*ᶜ*un* مَبْيُوعٌ which has a cluster of a vowelless *y* and *ū* becomes *mabu(ū)*ᶜ*un* مَبُوعٌ after that its

2nd radical *y* is elided. Then the ḍamma of the *b* is replaced by a kasra as an indication of the elided *y* so that it becomes *mabiū*$^c$*un* مَبِوعٌ. As there is in it a disliked combination of an *ū* preceded by a kasra, the *ū* is changed into an *ī* so that it becomes *mab(i)ī*$^c$*un* مَبِيعٌ. So according to his theory, *mab(i)ī*$^c$*un* مَبِيعٌ is formed according to *maf(i)īlun* مَفِيلٌ.

An analysis of both these theories shows that according to Sībawaihi's, it is the infixed *ū* that is elided from *mabuyū*$^c$*un* مَبْيُوْعٌ before that the other changes are carried out in it whereas according to al-Aḫfaš it is the 2nd radical *y* that is elided. As for the reasons why the infixed segment is elided in the first case and the radical in the other, they are the same as those concerning *maqwuwlun / maqw(u)ūlun* مَقْوُوْلٌ (cf. par. 20).

## 38.2 In the verb with 3rd weak radical:

The conjugation *fa*$^c$*ula* فَعُلَ does not exit in the verb with 3rd radical *y* due to the dislike of having the 3rd radical y following a ḍamma (cf. Ibn Ğinnī, *Munṣif I,* 244, Hindāwī, *Manāhiğ* 354).

The only conjugations of the class of verb with 3rd weak *y* can be grouped into the following:

1- *fa<sup>c</sup>ala yaf<sup>c</sup>ilu* فَعَلَ يفْعِلُ, e.g. *ramaya yarmiyu* رَمَيَ يرْمِيُ "to throw" that becomes after the phonological change *ram(a)ā yarm(i)ī* رَمَي يرْمِي.

2- *fa<sup>c</sup>ala yaf<sup>c</sup>alu* فَعَلَ يَفْعَلُ, e.g. *nahaya yanhayu* نَهَيَ يَنْهَيُ "to forbid" that becomes after the phonological change *nah(a)ā yanh(a)ā* نَهَى يَنْهَى.

3- *fa<sup>c</sup>ila yaf<sup>c</sup>alu* فَعِلَ يفْعَلُ, e.g. *raḍiya yarḍayu* رَضِيَ يَرْضَيُ "to consent" that becomes after the phonological change *raḍ(a)ā yarḍ(a)ā* رَضَى يرْضَى.

### <u>*38.2.1 At the end of the word:*</u>

The verb with 3rd *y* radical *raḍiya* رَضِيَ "he consented" is conformable to the conjugation *fa<sup>c</sup>ila yaf<sup>c</sup>alu* فَعِلَ يفْعَلُ. It is originally *raḍiwa* رَضِوَ with the 3rd vowelled radical *w* changed into a y on account of the influence of the kasra preceding it (cf.

Lane, I, 1099). This means that *raḍiy(u)ū* رَضِيُوا "they consented /masc. pl" is originally *raḍiw(u)ū* رَضِوُوا with the 3rd vowelled radical *w* changed into a *y* due to the influence of the kasra preceding it. Then as the ḍamma that vowels the *y* in *raḍiy(u)ū* رَضِيُوا is deemed as heavy, it is shifted to the *ḍ*, i.e. *raḍuy(u)ū* رَضُيُوا , which causes a cluster of two vowelless letters, the vowelless *y* and *w* (cf. Ibn Ǧinnī, Munṣif II, 126). So the *y* is elided and it became *raḍ(u)ū* رَضُوا (cf. further Åkesson, *Ibn Mas*ᶜ*ūd,* the Commentary (49), (275), (303)).

*38.3 In the doubled weak verb:*

An example is *ḥayiya* حَيِيَ "to live" that did not become *ḥ(a)āya* حَايَ, to avoid that its imperfect becomes *yaḥ(a)āyu* يَحَايُ (cf. Åkesson, *Ibn Mas*ᶜ*ūd* 284: fol. 28a), with the disliked combination of the ḍamma vowelling the *y*.

A closer look at *ḥayiya* حَيِيَ "to live"shows that it has the sequence *yi* that is not changed into *(a)ā* due to the influence of the fatḥa preceding it, namely *ḥ(a)āya* حَايَ, in order to avoid that its imperfect becomes *yaḥ(a)āyu* يَحَايُ, with the disliked combination of the ḍamma following the *y* that is deemed as heavy (cf. Åkesson, *Conversion* 28 and par. 26.2.1 of this study). Instead the imperfect is *yaḥy(a)ā* [with final *alif maqṣūra]* يَحْيَى.

### 39- The *w* or *y* vowelled by a fatḥa and preceded by a vowelless consonant has its vowel shifted

Some examples are the verb with 2nd radical *w* formed according to the conjugation *yafᶜalu* that occurs in the imperfect, e.g. *yaḫwafu* يَخْوَفُ that becomes *yaḫawfu* يَخَوْفُ and then *yaḫ(a)āfu* يَخافُ "he is afraid", the imperfect of the passive voice of the verb with 2nd radical *w* or *y* formed according to *yufᶜalu* يُفْعَلُ, e.g. *yuqwalu* يُقْوَلُ “it is said” that becomes *yuqawlu* يُقَوْلُ and then *yuq(a)ālu* يُقَالُ "is said" and *yubyaᶜu* يُبْيَعُ that becomes *yubayᶜu* يُبَيْعُ and then *yub(a)āᶜu* يُبَاعُ "is sold" and the noun of place of a verb with 2nd radical *w*, e.g. *maqwalun* مَقْوَلٌ that becomes *maqawlun* مَقَوْلٌ and then *maq(a)ālun* مَقَالٌ "speech".

Another example is the verb with 2nd radical *y* that is formed according to the conjugation *yaf<sup>c</sup>ilu* يَفْعِلُ in the imperfect, e.g. *yabyi<sup>c</sup>u* يَبْيِعُ > *yabiy<sup>c</sup>u* يَبِيْعُ > *yab(i)ī<sup>c</sup>u* يَبِيعُ "he sells".

*39.1 The w or y remains sound:*

The *w* or *y* remains sound in *ǧadwalun* جَدْوَلٌ "a rivulet" (cf. Åkesson, *Ibn Mas<sup>c</sup>ūd* 286: fol. 29a, Howell, IV, fasc. I, 1524), in which the *w* is vowelled by a fatḥa and preceded by a sukūn, from *ǧadala* جَدَلَ "to make firm". The reason of the *w's* soundness in it is that the noun is quasi-coordinate to the measure *fa<sup>c</sup>walun* فَعْوَلٌ and hence is not formed according to the verbal *fa<sup>c</sup>al* فَعَلَ. So the *w* could not be changed into an *ā* after that its fatḥa is shifted to the *ǧ* preceding it, i.e. *ǧad(a)ālun* جَدَالٌ, as this would cancel the formation.

Other examples are *miqwalun* مِقْوَلٌ "loquacious, eloquent" that is contracted from the base form *miqw(a)ālun* مِقْوَالٌ "loquacious, eloquent" with 2nd radical *w*, and *miḫyaṭun* مِخْيَطٌ "a needle" that is contracted from the base form *miḫy(a)āṭun* مِخْيَاطٌ "a needle" (cf. Åkesson, *Ibn Mas<sup>c</sup>ūd* 288: fol. 29a) with

2nd radical *y*. So the pattern *mif*ᶜ*alun* مفْعَلٌ is the contracted form of *mif*ᶜ*(a)ālun* مفْعَالٌ.

**40- The vowelless *w* preceded by or preceding a kasra is changed into a *y* and the y is not changed into a *w***

An example is *miwz(a)ānun* مِوْزَانٌ with the *w* preceded by a kasra that becomes *m(i)yz(a)ānun* مِيْزَانٌ with the *w* changed into a *y* and then *m(i)īz(a)ānun* مِيزَانٌ "balancc".

Another example is *mawyitun* مَوْيِتٌ "a dead man", in which the vowelless 2nd radical *w* precedes the *y* vowelled by a kasra. The result is the change of the *w* into a *y* and the assimilation of the *y* to the *y*. Thus *mawyitun* مَوْيِتٌ becomes *mayyitun* مَيِّتٌ after that the *w* is changed into a *y* and the yāᵓs are assimilated.

Both variants *maytun* مَيْتٌ and *mayyitun* مَيِّتٌ are combined in this verse said by ᶜAdī b. al-Raᶜlā, cited by Muᵓaddib, *Taṣrīf* 113, 268, Ibn Yaᶜīš, X, 69, *Mulūkī* 466, Ibn Manẓūr, VI, 4295, Howell, IV, fasc. I, 1461, Åkesson, *Ibn Mas*ᶜ*ūd* 301: (264):

"لَيْسَ مَنْ مَاتَ فَاسْتَرَاحَ بِمَيْتٍ إِنَّمَا الْمَيْتُ مَيِّتُ الأَحْيَاءِ".

*"Laysa man māta fa-starāḥa bi-maytin*
*ʾinnamā l-maytu mayyitu l-ʾaḥyāʾi".*
"He who has died, and taken his rest, is not
really dead:
the really dead is only the dead of the living, [i.e.
is only he that is living, while his state is like that
of the dead]".

**41- The alleviation of the hamza**

The reason of the alleviation of the hamza in many cases is that it is a hard heavy consonant uttered from the farthest part of the throat.

*41.1 At the beginning of a word when following another word ending with a vowel:*

The alleviation of the hamza is regular when it concerns the connective hamza following a vowel in the word preceding it, as it becomes a *waṣla* (for discussions see Wright, I, 19-20). An example is the hamza vowelled by a fatḥa, *ʾa,* of the definite article *-ʾal* that becomes *-l* after the alleviation with the *waṣla,* e.g. *bintu r-r(a)ā<sup>c</sup>(i)ī* بِنْتُ ٱلرّاعي said instead of *bintu ʾal- r-r(a)āᶜ(i)ī* بِنْتُ ألرّاعي "the shepherd's daughter".

The alleviation of the hamza can be considered as anomalous in other cases. Some anomalous examples are *ʾun(a)āsun* أُنَاسٌ that becomes after the elision of the hamza *n(a)āsun* نَاسٌ "people" (cf. Ibn Ǧinnī, *Ḫaṣāʾiṣ III,* 151, Ibn Manẓūr, I, 147, Howell, I, fasc. I, 174, Fleisch, *Traité I,* 151) and *al-ʾil(a)āhu* الإِلَه that becomes after the elision of the hamza *al-l(a)āhu* اللّهُ (cf. Åkesson, *Ibn Masᶜūd* 242-243: fol. 23a, Ibn Manẓūr, I, 114).

**42- The combination of two hamzas is deemed as heavy**

*42.1 At the beginning of the word:*

The hamza that is vowelless and preceded by a hamza vowelled by a fatḥa at the initial of the word is changed into an *ā,* and hence the hamza is assimilated to the *ā* resulting in a madda. Some examples that can be mentioned are those formed according to the pattern *ʾafᶜalu* أَفْعَلُ, e.g. *ʾaʾḫaḏu* أَأْخَذُ "the one who holds mostly against" that becomes *ʾ(a)āḫaḏu* آخَذُ and

*ʾaʾdamu* أَأْدَمُ "tawny, dark-complexioned" that becomes *ʾ(a)ādamu* آدَمُ with the *madda* as their initial segment (cf. Sībawaihi, II, 174, Ibn Ǧinnī, *Sirr II,* 579, 665, Åkesson, *Ibn Masᶜūd* 242: fol. 22b).

An anomalous case that can be mentioned is the plural of *ʾimāmun* إِمَامٌ "imam", which is *ʾayimmatun* أيِمَّةٌ originally *ʾaʾmimatun* أأْمِمَةٌ with the hamza that is vowelless and preceded by a hamza vowelled by a fatḥa. The 2nd hamza is changed into *y* for the purpose of alleviation and the kasra of the *m* is shifted to it, namely *ʾayimmatun* أيِمَّةٌ (cf. Zamaḫšarī, 167, Ibn Manẓūr, I, 133, Howell, IV, fasc. I 971 sqq., Lane, I, 91, Vernier, I, 101), because the combination of two hamzas at the initial of the word is deemed as heavy.

The Kufans however maintain anomalously both the hamzas at the initial of the word, as they recite the sur. 9: 12 as *(fa-qātilū ʾaʾimmata l-kufri)* فَقَاتِلُوا أَإِمَّةَ الْكُفْرِ "Fight ye the chiefs of Unfaith", with *ʾaʾimmata* أَإِمَّةَ read instead of *ʾayimmata* أيِمَّة (cf. Ibn Ḫālawaihi, *Qirāʾāt I,* 235, Åkesson, *Ibn Masᶜūd* 242: fol. 22b). This reading is disliked by Ibn Ǧinnī (cf. Ibn Ǧinnī, *Ḫaṣāʾiṣ III,* 143, *Sirr I,* 81).

*42.1.1 The hamza is vowelless and preceded by a hamza vowelled by a ḍamma:*

The hamza that is vowelless and preceded by a hamza vowelled by a ḍamma is in most cases changed into a *w*. An example in which such a combination is carried out at the initial of the word is the passive voice of Form IV of *ʾaṯara* أَثَرَ "to report" in the 3rd person of the masc. sing. formed according to *f(u)ūʿila*, namely *ʾuʾṯira* أُأْثِرَ "it was reported" with the 2nd vowelless hamza preceded by a ḍamma. It becomes *ʾ(u)wṯira* أُوْثِرَ with the hamza changed into a *w*, then as the vowelless *w* in it is preceded by a ḍamma, it becomes *ʾ(u)ūṯira* أُوثِرَ "he, or it was preferred /(passive)" with the *w* assimilated to the ḍamma resulting in the lengthened *ū* (cf. Åkesson, *Ibn Masʿūd* 242: fol. 22b-23a).

However it can be observed that in some cases of 1st radical hamzated verbs of the conjugation *faʿala yafʿulu* فَعَلَ يَفْعُلُ occurring in the imperative according to *ʾufʿul* اُفْعُلْ, e.g. *ʾuʾḫuḏ* أُأْخُذْ "take!" and *ʾuʾkul* أُأْكُلْ "eat!" with the 2nd vowelless hamza preceded by the hamza of the imperative vowelled by a ḍamma, both hamzas are elided resulting respectively in *ḫuḏ* خُذْ and *kul* كُلْ (cf. Ibn Ğinnī, *de Flexione* 33, Åkesson, *Ibn Mas*ᶜ*ūd* 242: fol. 23a, Howell, II-III, 89-90, IV, fasc. I, 957-958, Wright, II, 76, Vernier, I, 103).

The elision of the hamza is obligatory in *ḫuḏ* خُذْ which is not to be said *ʾuʾḫuḏ* أأْخُذْ with the combination of both hamzas, or *ʾuwḫuḏ* أُوخُذْ with the change of the 2nd hamza into a *w*, and in *kul* كُلْ which is not to be said *ʾuʾkul* أأْكُلْ, *ʾuwkul* or *ʾ(u)ūkul* أوكُلْ. The elision however is not necessary in *murr* مُرْ which is allowed, as well as in *ʾuʾmur* أُأْمُرْ in which the 1st hamza is maintained and the 1st radical hamza is changed into a *w* resulting in *ʾ(u)ūmur* أُومُرْ. Also *ʾamur* أمُرْ with the vowelling of the hamza with a fatḥa occurs as in the sur. 20: 132 *(wa-ʾamur ʾahlaka bi-l-ṣalwati)* وَأمُرْ أهلَكَ بالصَلٰوات "Enjoin prayer on thy people" and in the sur. 7: 199 *(wa-ʾamur bi-l-*ᶜ*urfi ḫuḏi l-*ᶜ*afwa)* وَأمُرْ بِالْعُرفِ خُذِ العَفْوَ "Hold to forgiveness; Command what is right".

*42.1.2 The hamza is vowelless and preceded by a hamza vowelled by a kasra:*

The hamza that is vowelless and preceded by a hamza vowelled by a kasra is changed into a *y*. An example in which such a combination occurs is the imperative of the 2nd person of the masc. sing. of a verb with 1st hamza radical *ʾasara* أَسَرَ "to capture", namely *ʾiʾsir* إِئْسِرْ "capture! /2 masc. sing." with the 2nd vowelless hamza preceded by a kasra which becomes *ʾ(i)ysir* إِيْسِرْ with the *ʾ* changed into a *y*, and as the vowelless *y* in it is preceded by a kasra, it becomes *ʾ(i)īsir* إِيسِرْ with the *y* assimilated to the kasra resulting in the lengthened *ī* (cf. Åkesson, *Ibn Masʿūd* 242: fol. 22b)

*42.1.3 Both hamzas are vowelled by a fatha in one word or in two words following each other:*

Two hamzas vowelled by a fatḥa combined together can occur in one word or in two words following each other.

The possible assimilation of two hamzas vowelled by a fatḥa following each other at the beginning of the word concerns some examples in which the interrogative particle, *ʾa*, is prefixed in a word which has the conjunctive hamza vowelled by the fatḥa of the definite *ᵓal-* attached to it, e.g. *ᵓa-ᵓal-Ḥasanu ᶜindaka* أأَلْحَسنُ عِنْدَكَ "Is al-Ḥasan by you?" which becomes *ᵓ(a)āl-Ḥasanu ᶜindaka* آلْحَسنُ عِنْدَكَ.

The anomalous insertion of the *ā* in words in which the initial segment is the conjunctive hamza *ᵓa,* to which the interrogative particle, *ᵓa,* is prefixed to, can be remarked, e.g. *ᵓa-ᵓanti* أأَنْتِ "Are you /fem. sing.?" which becomes *ᵓ(a)ā-ᵓanti* آنْتِ (cf. Sībawaihi, II, 173, Åkesson, *Ibn Masᶜūd* 242: fol. 23a).

As an example, the anomalous *ᵓ(a)ā-ᵓanti* that occurs in this part of a verse said by D̲ū l-Rumma, cited by Sībawaihi, II, 173, Ibn Ǧinnī, *Sirr II,* 723, Muᵓaddib, *Taṣrīf* 32, Zamaḫšarī, 14, 167, Ibn Yaᶜīš, IX, 118-120, Howell, I, fasc. I, 119, IV, fasc. I, 982, Åkesson, *Ibn Masᶜūd* 262: (233) can be mentioned:

"فَيَا ظَبْيَةَ الْوَعْسَاءِ بَيْنَ جُلاجِلٍ وَبَيْنَ النَّقَا آأَنْتِ أَمْ أُمُّ سَالِمٍ".

*"Fa-yā ẓabyata l-waᶜsāᵓi bayna ǧulāǧilin*
*wa-bayna l-naqā ᵓāᵓanti ᵓam ᵓummu Sālimin"*
"Then, O gazelle of the soft sandy ground

between Ǧulāǧil
and the sand-hill, is this really you or Umm Sālim?".

Such a sequence occurs when the hamza, which is the initial letter of a word, is vowelled by a fatḥa and is preceded by a hamza vowelled by a fatḥa in the word preceding it (cf. Sībawaihi, II, 172, Zamaḫšarī, 167, Åkesson, *Ibn Mas*ᶜ*ūd* 242: fol. 23a, Howell, IV, fasc. I, 983-986).

An example is the sur. 47: 18 *(fa-qad ǧā*ᵓ*a* ᵓ*ašrāṭuhā)* فَقَدْ جاءَ أشرَاطُها "But already Have come some tokens", in which *ǧā*ᵓ*a* ᵓ*ašrāṭuhā* جاءَ أشرَاطُها presents a combination of two hamzas vowelled by a fatḥa. Al-Ḫalīl and some other Arabs alleviate the 2nd hamza and not the 1st one, and recite it as *fa-qad ǧā*ᵓ*a šrāṭuhā* فَقَدْ جاءَ آشرَاطُها whereas the Ḥiǧāzīs alleviate both the hamzas by eliding the 1st one and changing the 2nd one into a *waṣla,* namely *fa-qad ǧā šrāṭuhā* فَقَدْ جا آشراطُها (cf. Åkesson, *Ibn Mas*ᶜ*ūd* 242: fol. 23a).

<u>*42.2 At the middle of the word:*</u>

The combination of both hamzas at the middle of the word is more permitted. An example is *ḫaṭā*ᵓ*i*ᵓ*ī* خَطائئي "my sins" used instead of *ḫaṭāyāya* خَطايايا in the sentence *ʾallahumma ġfir lī ḫaṭāʾiī* اللّهُمَّ اْغفِرْ لِي خَطَائئي "O God forgive me my sins", which according to Zamaḫšarī, 167, Abū Zaid has heard from Abū l-Samḥ and his cousin Raddād.

**43- The alleviation of the hamza by its change into a glide or its elision***:*

The hamza can be found in a sequence in which it occurs vowelless and the segment preceding it can be vowelled by a fatḥa, a ḍamma or a kasra. In all these three cases the hamza can be maintained or alleviated. In the latter case, it is changed into a glide of the same nature of the vowel of the segment preceding it (cf. Åkesson, *Ibn Masʿūd* 240: fol. 21b, Roman, *Étude I,* 330).

*43.1 The hamza is vowelless and preceded by a vowel:*

If the hamza is vowelless and preceded by a segment vowelled by a fatḥa, the hamza is changed into an *ā.* An example is *raʾsun* رَأْسٌ with the vowelless *ʾ* preceded by a fatḥa that becomes *r(a)āsun* رَاسٌ "a head" after the change of the *ʾ* into *ā.*

If the segment preceding the hamza is vowelled by a ḍamma the hamza is changed into an *ū*. An example is *luᵓmun* لُؤْمٌ with the vowelless ᵓ preceded by a ḍamma that becomes *l(u)ūmun* لُومٌ "blame" after the change of the ᵓ into *ū*.

If the segment preceding the hamza is vowelled by a kasra the hamza is changed into an *ī*. An example is *biᵓrun* بِئْرٌ with the vowelless ᵓ preceded by a kasra that becomes *b(i)īrun* بِيرٌ "well, spring" after the change of the ᵓ into *ī*.

<u>*43.2 The hamza is vowelled and preceded by a vowel:*</u>

The hamza that is vowelled by one of the three vowels and preceded by a fatḥa can be changed into a *hamza bayna bayna* "intermediary hamza" (cf. Sībawaihi, II, 168-169, Åkesson, *Ibn Masᶜūd* 240: 21b, Roman, 324-326, Lane, I, 288).

If the hamza's vowel is a fatḥa, then the glide that it is connected to is the *ā*, e.g. *s(a)āla* سَالَ from *saᵓala* سَأَلَ "to ask".

An example concerning the hamza alleviated for the sake of metric exigency, is the verb with 3rd radical hamza *hanaᵓaki* هَنَأَكِ that is said *han(a)āki* هَنَاكِ (cf. Åkesson, *Ibn Masᶜūd* 240:

fol. 22a) in a verse composed by Farazdaq, which is cited by Sībawaihi, II, 175, Ibn Ǧinnī, *Ḫaṣā'iṣ III,* 152, *Sirr II,* 666, Ibn al-Sarrāǧ, *Uṣūl III,* 469, Mu'addib, *Taṣrīf* 530, Zamaḫšarī, 166, Ibn Yaᶜīš, IX, 113, *Mulūkī* 229, Ibn ᶜUṣfūr, I, 405, Howell, IV, fasc. I, 951, Åkesson, *Ibn Masᶜūd* 255: (220). It runs as follows:

"رَاحَتْ بِمَسلَمَةَ الْبِغَالُ عَشِيّةَ فَارْعَى فَزَارَةُ لا هَنَاكِ الْمَرْتَعُ".

*"Rāḥat bi-Maslamata l-biġālu ᶜašiyyata*
*fa-rᶜā Fazāratu lā hanāki l-martaᶜu"*
"The mules have gone away with Maslama at
evening.
Then graze your camels, Fazāra. May the pasture not
be pleasant to you!".

If the hamza's vowel is a ḍamma then the glide that it is connected to is a *w,* e.g. *lawuma* لَوُمَ from *la'uma* لَؤُمَ "he was base" and if it is a kasra then the glide that it is connected to is a *y,* e.g. *sayima* سَيِمَ from *sa'ima* سَئِمَ "he was weary".

If the hamza is vowelled by a kasra and is preceded by a fatḥa, it can be changed into a *y* vowelled by a kasra.

If the segment preceding the hamza vowelled by a fatḥa is a ḍamma, the hamza can be changed into a *w*. An example is *guʾanun* جُؤَنٌ "receptable for bottles or the like" that becomes *ğuwanun* جُوَنٌ with the change of the ʾ into a *w* (cf. Zamaḫšarī, 174, Ibn Ğinnī, *Sirr II,* 573, Åkesson, *Ibn Masʿūd* 240: 21b).

If the segment preceding the hamza is a kasra, the hamza can be changed into a *y*. An example is *miʾarun* مِئَرٌ "exciting dissension among the people" that becomes *miyarun* مِيَرٌ with the change of the ʾ into a *y* (cf. Sībawaihi, II, 169, Zamaḫšarī, 166, Åkesson, *Ibn Masʿūd* 240: fol. 21b).

If the hamza is vowelled by a fatḥa and is preceded by a vowelless segment, it can be elided and its fatḥa is shifted to the segment preceding it (cf. Åkesson, *Ibn Masʿūd* 240-242: fols. 22a-22b).

The strong vowelless segment preceding the hamza vowelled by a fatḥa can be the *l*- of the definite article, *al-,* or a radical. The change procedure is that the hamza's fatḥa is shifted to the vowelless strong segment and the hamza is elided.

An example in which the segment preceding the hamza is the vowelless *l-* of the definite article is *al-ʾaḥmaru* الأَحْمَرُ "red" with the *l-* of the definite article, *al-*, vowelless preceding the hamza vowelled by a fatḥa. This sequence leads to the elision of the hamza and the transfer of its fatḥa to the *l* preceding it, namely *ʾalaḥmaru* الَحْمَرُ. Another variant exists as well, namely *laḥmar* لَحْمَرُ with the hamza of the article elided (cf. Sībawaihi, II, 170, Zamaḫšarī, 166-167, Åkesson, *Ibn Masᶜūd* 240: fol. 22a, Howell, IV, fasc. I, 942-943, 959-963, Lane, I, 74, Wright, II, 269).

Some examples in which the segment preceding the hamza is a radical is the imperfect with the 2nd radical hamza *yasʾalu* يَسْأَلُ "he asks" that becomes anomalously *yasalu* يَسَلُ and its *maṣdar masʾalatun* مَسْأَلَةٌ "a matter" that becomes *masalatun* مَسَلَةٌ (cf. Zamaḫšarī, 166, Åkesson, *Ibn Masᶜūd* 240: fol. 22a). In both these examples the 1st radical *s* is vowelless and precedes the hamza vowelled by a fatḥa. As it has been observed, this sequence results in the elision of the hamza and the transfer of its fatḥa to the *s* preceding it.

Another example is *malʾakun* مَلْأَكٌ "angel" (from *ʾalaka* أَلَكَ "to convey") with the 2nd radical *l* vowelless, preceding the hamza vowelled by a fatḥa. This sequence results in the elision of the hamza and the transfer of its fatḥa to the *l* preceding it, namely *malakun* مَلَكٌ (cf. Ibn Ğinnī, *Munṣif II*, 102-104, Ibn Manẓūr, I, 110-111, Åkesson, *Ibn Masᶜūd* 240: fol. 22a, Wright, II, 77, Vernier, I, 101-102, Lane, I, 81-82).

The vowelless segment preceding the hamza vowelled by a fatḥa in the same word can be an infixed glide, namely a *w* or a *y*. The conditions of the hamza's elision and consequently of the transfer of its fatḥa to the segment preceding it, is that the infixed segment is not a segment of prolongation, i.e. a glide lengthening the sound of the vowel preceding it, as the *w* in *mafᶜuwlatun (/ mafᶜ(u)ūlatun)* مَفْعُولَةٌ that lengthens the ḍamma preceding it, or the *y* in *faᶜiylatun (/ faᶜ(i)īlatun)* فَعِيلَةٌ that lengthens the kasra preceding it and that the infixed segment is not specific for the diminutive, as the *y* in *ʾufayʾilun* أُفَيْعِلٌ, because in these cases the hamza is assimilated to the glide preceding it.

If the segment preceding the hamza is a vowelless *w,* the hamza is elided and its fatḥa is transferred to the *w* preceding it.

An example *is ǧawʾabatun* جَوْأَبَةٌ *"Ǧawʾaba* [name of a water]", which is from the root *ǧ ʾ b* جَأَبَ (cf. Howell, IV, fasc. I, 938), in which the infixed *w* is there to make it identical to the pattern *fawᶜalatun* فَوْعَلَةٌ.

If the segment preceding the hamza is a vowelless *y,* the hamza is elided and its fatḥa is transferred to the *y* preceding it. An example is *ǧayʾalun* جَيْأَلٌ "female hyena", which is from the root *ǧ ʾ l* جَأَلَ (cf. Ibn Manẓūr, I, 529, Lane, I, 370), in which the infixed *y* is added to make it identical to the pattern *fayᶜalun* فَيْعَلٌ.

If the infixed segment is a vowelless *w* as the *w* in *mafᶜ(u)wlatun (/ mafᶜ(u)ūlatun)* مَفْعُولَةٌ lengthening the ḍamma preceding it, the hamza vowelled by a fatḥa is alleviated by its change into the same segment as the segment preceding it, which is a *w,* and then an assimilation of the wāws is carried out. An example is *maqruwʾatun (> maqr(u)ūʾatun)* مَقْرُوءَةٌ "a writing read" which is formed according to the pattern *mafᶜuwlatun* مَفْعُولَةٌ with the infixed prolonged *w* lengthening the sound of the ḍamma preceding it. The hamza vowelled by a fatḥa is alleviated by its change into the same segment as the segment preceding it, which is a *w*, and then an assimilation of the wāws is carried out resulting in *maqruwwatun* مقْروَّةٌ (for discussions see Sībawaihi, II, 171, 175, Åkesson, *Ibn Mas*ᶜ*ūd* 242: fols. 22a-22b, Howell, IV, fasc. I, 936-937, de Sacy, I, 370, Vernier, I, 102, 350).

If the infixed segment is a vowelless *y* as the *y* in *fa*ᶜ*iylatun* (/ *fa*ᶜ*(i)īlatun)* فعيلَةٌ lengthening the kasra preceding it, the hamza vowelled by a fatḥa is alleviated by its change into the same segment as the segment preceding it, namely a *y*, and then an assimilation of the yāʾs is carried out. An example is *ḫaṭiyʾatun* (> *ḫaṭ(i)īʾatun)* خطيئَةٌ "an error, sin", which is formed according to the pattern *fa*ᶜ*iylatun* فَعيلَةٌ with the infixed *y* lengthening the sound of the kasra preceding it. The hamza vowelled by a fatḥa is alleviated by its change into the same segment as the segment preceding it, namely a *y*, and then an assimilation of the yāʾs is carried out resulting in *ḫaṭ(i)yyatun* خطيَّةٌ (for discussions see Sībawaihi, II, 171, 175, Åkesson, *Ibn Mas*ᶜ*ūd* 242: fol. 22a-22b, Howell, IV, fasc. I, 936-937, de Sacy, I, 370, Vernier, I, 102, 350, O'Leary, *Semitic Languages* 36).

If the infixed segment is a vowelless *y* as the *y* in *ᵓufayᶜilun* أُفَيْعِلٌ, which is specific for the diminutive, the hamza vowelled by a kasra is alleviated by its change into the same segment as the segment preceding it, namely the *y*, and then an assimilation of the yāᵓs is carried out. An example is *ᵓufayᵓisun* أُفَيْئِسٌ "a kind of little hoe, a little axe", which is formed according to the pattern *ᵓufayᵓilun* أُفَيْئِلٌ, in which the hamza vowelled by a kasra is alleviated by its change into the same segment as the segment preceding it, namely a *y*, and then an assimilation of the yāᵓs is carried out resulting in *ᵓufayyisun* أُفَيِّسٌ (for discussions see Sībawaihi, II, 171, 175, Åkesson, *Ibn Masᶜūd* 242: fol. 22a-22b, Howell, IV, fasc. I, 936-937, de Sacy, I, 370, Vernier, I, 102, 350).

If the infixed segment is a vowelless *ā* of prolongation as in the active participle *f(a)āᶜilun* فَاعِلٌ and the broken pl. of the nouns *maf(a)āᶜilun* مَفَاعِلٌ in which the alif lengthens the sound of the fatḥa preceding it, the hamza vowelled by a kasra is alleviated by its change into a *hamza bayna bayna* (for discussions see Sībawaihi, II, 171, Roman, *Étude I,* 333). Some examples that are formed according to the active participle *f(a)āᶜilun* فَاعِلٌ are *s(a)āᵓilun* سَائِلٌ "a questioner" with the 2nd radical hamza vowelled by a kasra, from *saᵓala* "to ask", which results after the change of the hamza into a *hamza bayna bayna* in *s(a)āyilun* سَايِلٌ, and *q(a)āᵓilun* قَائِلٌ "a teller" from *q(a)āwilun* قَاوِلٌ with the 2nd radical *w* changed into a hamza vowelled by a kasra, from *qawala* "to tell", which results after the change in *q(a)āyilun* قَايِلٌ (cf. Åkesson, *Ibn Masᶜūd* 242: fol. 22b). An example that is formed according to the broken pl. of the nouns *maf(a)āᶜilun* مَفَاعِلُ is *mas(a)āᵓilun* مَسَائِلُ "questions" (cf. Sībawaihi, II, 171, Roman, *Étude I*, 333) which results in *mas(a)āyilun* مَسَايِلُ.

<u>*43.3 In two words:*</u>

The elision of the hamza that is vowelled by a fatḥa is as well carried out if the vowelless *w, y* or the strong segment preceding it, is not in the same word as the hamza. In this case the vowelled hamza, which is the initial segment of the second word, is elided, and its vowel, the fatḥa, is shifted to the vowelless segment preceding it which is the ultimate segment of the word preceding it (for a study see Sībawaihi, II, 171-172,

Zamaḫšarī, 166, Åkesson, *Ibn Masᶜūd* 240-242: fol. 22a,
Howell, IV, fasc. I, 938 sqq., Vernier, I, 104).

An example is *ᵓAbuw ᵓAyyūba* أَبُو أَيّوبَ "the father of Job",
with the *w* vowelless in *ᵓAbuw (ᵓAb(u)ū)* أَبُو, marking its
nominative's ending as it is the 1st element of the construct state,
which precedes the hamza vowelled by a fatḥa that is the initial
segment of the second word. This sequence results in the elision
of the hamza from *ᵓAyyūba* and the transfer of its fatḥa to the *w*
preceding it, namely *ᵓAbuwa yyūba* أَبُو يّوبَ (cf. Åkesson, *Ibn
Masᶜūd* 240-242: fol. 22a, Howell, IV, fasc. I, 940).

Some other examples with the alleviation of the hamza, just to
mention a few, are *ḏuw ᵓamrihim* ذُو أَمْرِهِمْ "the author of their
matter" which becomes *ḏuwa mrihim* ذُوَ مُرِهِمْ (Ibn Yaᶜīš, IX,
109) and *q(a)āḍuw ᵓab(i)īka* قَاضُو أَبِيكَ "the judges of your
father" which becomes *qāḍuwa bīka* قَاضُوَ بِيكَ (cf. Ibn Yaᶜīš,
IX, 110, Howell, IV, fasc. I, 940).

If the vowelless weak ultimate segment in the word preceding
the hamza vowelled by a fatḥa is a *y,* the hamza is elided and its
fatḥa is transferred to the y preceding it.

An example is *ʾabtaġiy ʾamrahu* أَبْتَغِي أَمْرَهُ "I seek for his matter" with the *y* vowelless occuring as the 3rd radical of the first word *ʾabtaġiy* أَبْتَغِي, - which is the imperfect of the 1st person of the sing. of *baġiya* بَغِيَ -, preceding the hamza vowelled by a fatḥa that is the first initial segment of the second word, *ʾamrahu* أَمْرَهُ. This sequence results in the elision of the hamza from *ʾamrahu* أَمْرَهُ and the transfer of its fatḥa to the *y* preceding it, namely *ʾabtaġiya mrahu* أَبْتَغِيَ مْرَهُ (cf. Åkesson, *Ibn Masʿūd* 240-242: fol. 22a, Howell, IV, fasc. I, 940).

If the vowelless ultimate segment in the word preceding the hamza vowelled by a fatḥa is a strong segment, the hamza is elided and its fatḥa is transferred to the letter preceding it.

An example is *man ʾab(u)ūka* مَنْ أَبُوكَ with the strong letter, the *n*, vowelless occurring as the ultimate segment of the first word, namely the interrogative particle *man* مَنْ, preceding the hamza vowelled by a fatḥa that is the first initial segment of the second word, *ʾab(u)ūka* أَبُوكَ. This sequence results in the elision of the hamza from *ʾab(u)ūka* أَبُوكَ and the transfer of its fatḥa to the *n* preceding it, namely *mana būka* مَنَ بُوكَ "who is your father?" (cf. Ibn Yaᶜīš, IX, 110, Howell, IV, fasc. I, 940, Roman, *Étude I,* 332).

Another example is *qad ᵓaflaḥa* قَدْ أفْلَحَ of the sur. 23: 1 *(qad ᵓaflaḥa l-muᵓminūna)* قَدْ أفْلَحَ الْمُؤْمِنُونَ "The Believers must (eventually) win through", in which the strong segment, the *d,* of the first word, namely the particle *qad* قَدْ, is vowelless and precedes the hamza vowelled by a fatḥa that is the initial segment of the second word, namely the verb in the Form IV *ᵓaflaḥa* أفْلَحَ. This sequence results in the alleviation of the hamza from *ᵓaflaḥa* أفْلَحَ in the reading of some, by methods of eliding it and shifting its vowel to the segment preceding it, namely *qada flaḥa l-muᵓminūna* قَدَ ٱفْلَحَ الْمُؤْمِنُونَ (cf. Ibn Yaᶜīš, IX, 110).

Other examples, just to mention a few, are *law ᵓanna* لَوْ أنَّ that becomes *lawa nna* لَوَ ٱنَّ "if" and *qad ᵓaṣbaḥa* قَدْ أصبَحَ that becomes *qada ṣbaḥa* قَدَ ٱصبَحَ "he has become" (cf. Nöldeke, *Grammatik* 5).

If the hamza is vowelled by a ḍamma an preceded by an *ā* of prolongation, it is changed into a *hamza bayna bayna.* An example is *ǧazā(a)ᵓun* جَزَاءٌ "a recompense" that is formed according to the pattern *fa$^{c}$(a)ālun* فَعَالٌ in which the alif lengthens the sound of the fatḥa preceding it. It occurs in the sentence presented by Sībawaihi, II, 171 *ǧazā$^{\supset}$u $^{\supset}$ummihi* جَزَاءُ أُمّه "his mother's recompense". This hamza is changed into a *hamza bayna bayna* resulting in *ǧazāwu mmihi* جَزَاوُ أُمّه (cf. ibid, Roman, *Étude I,* 333).

**44- No phonological change can affect the initial weak letter of a word**

In words beginning with a weak letter, the weak letter remains usually sound in them. An example is *wa$^{c}$ada* وَعَدَ "to promise", in which the *w* remains sound on the basis that it is not preceded by any other segment. Hence, this means that the *w* in *wa$^{c}$ada* وَعَدَ cannot be made vowelless resulting in *w$^{c}$ada* وْعَدَ, because of the impossibility of beginning the word with a vowelless segment. It could not either be changed into *ā* resulting in *ā$^{c}$ada* اعَدَ as this would imply beginning the word with a vowelless segment which is forbidden, and it could not either be elided as the root would seem to be formed of two radicals, i.e. *ᶜada* عَدَ, which is not allowed (cf. Åkesson, *Ibn Masᶜūd* 270: fol. 25b-26a).

Other examples of verbs with the weak 1st radical retained in the perfect, are: *wahaba* وَهَبَ "he gave", *wağila* وَجِلَ "he was afraid", *wamiqa* وَمِقَ "he loved", *wabula* وَبُلَ "he was unwholesome".

It can be stated however, that the 1st weak radical can be elided in some cases of verbal nouns, e.g. *ᶜidatun* عِدَةٌ underlyingly *wiᶜdun* وِعْدٌ "a promise" (for some examples see Suyūṭī, *Muzhir II,* 158-159), in spite of the fact that it is the initial segment of the word. This opposes the rule that the glide should be preceded by another segment if a phonological change is to be carried out. The breaking of this rule requests however that the *tāᵓ marbūṭa* is suffixed to the word as a compensation for the elision of this initial glide (cf. Sībawaihi, II, 81, Wright, II, 118, Lane, II, 2952).

Not only the *tāᵓ marbūṭa* can occur as a compensation of a glide in the same word, but also another word, occurring as the 2nd element of an *ᵓiḍāfa* construction, can occur as a compensation for the elision of a *tāᵓ marbūṭa.* As an example to be mentioned, the *tāʾ marbūṭa* is anomalously elided from the accusative *ᶜidata* عِدَةَ which is said *ᶜida* عِدَ, when it occurs as the first element of a construct state in this verse said by Abū Umayya al-Faḍl b. al-ᶜAbbās b. ᶜUtba b. Abī Lahab, that is cited by Ibn Ǧinnī, *Ḫaṣāʾiṣ III,* 171, Muʾaddib, *Taṣrīf* 285, Suyūṭī, *Ašbāh III,* 248, Ibn Manẓūr, VI, 4871, Howell, I, fasc. IV, 1527-1528, IV, fasc. I, 1423-1424, Åkesson, *Ibn Masᶜūd* 277: (248):

"إِنَّ الْخَلِيطَ أَجَدُّوا الْبَيْنَ فَانْجَرَدُوا      وَأَخْلَفُوكَ عِدَ الأَمْرِ الَّذِي وَعَدُوا".

*"ʾInna l-ḫalīṭa ʾaǧaddū l-bayna fa-nǧara*
*wa-ʾaḫlafūka ᶜida l-ʾamri l-laḏī waᶜadū".*

"Verily the familiar friends have renewed the
separation, and made off,
and have broken to you the promise of the matter
which they promised".

**45- The combination of two phonological changes due to the unsound letters should be avoided**

An example that can introduce two phonological changes, which is forbidden, is the doubly weak verb *ṭawaya* طَوَيَ in which the sequence *ya* preceded by a fatḥa is changed into an *(a)ā,* namely *ṭaw(a)ā* [with final *alif maqṣūra]* طَوَى "to fold" (cf. Åkesson, *Ibn Mas*ᶜ*ūd* 284: fol. 28a). It is not allowed after this change to change the sequence *wa* of *ṭaw(a)ā* طَوَى preceded by a fatḥa into *(a)ā* that would result in *ṭ(a)āā* طَاى as this would necessarily imply a cluster of two vowelless glides, the alifs: the *alif mamdūda* and the *alif maqṣūra.*

It can be remarked that the phonological change is not carried out as well in the dual of the masc. *ṭaway(a)ā* طَوَيَا "/dual" in spite of the fact that the final radical *y* is vowelled, and thus there is no risk in combining two vowelless segments, by analogy with *ṭaw(a)ā* طَوَى (cf. ibid, 284: fol. 28a). In other words *ṭaway(a)ā* طَوَيَا could have become *ṭ(a)āy(a)ā* طَايَا, but did not do so by analogy with *ṭaw(a)ā* طَوَى that did not either become *ṭ(a)āā* طَاى.

**46- The combination of the ḍamma preceding the kasra is disliked**

There are no nouns of the pattern *fu*ᶜ*ilun* فُعِلٌ with the 1st radical vowelled by a ḍamma and the 2nd radical vowelled by a kasra, which offers a disliked combination, except *wu*ᶜ*ilun* وُعِلٌ "a mountain goat" and *du*ᵓ*ilun* دُئِلٌ "a jackal" (cf. Ibn Manẓūr, VI, 4875, Åkesson, *Ibn Mas*ᶜ*ūd,* the Commentary (133).

The noun *du*ᵓ*ilun* دُئِلٌ is also used as a name for a tribe of Kināna (cf. Ibn Manẓūr, II, 1313). It occurs as well in this verse said by Kaᶜb b. Mālik al-Anṣārī describing the army of Abū Sufyān, when he made a raid upon al-Madīna. It is cited by Ibn Ǧinnī, *Munṣif I,* 20, Ibn Yaᶜīš, *Mulūkī* 24, Ibn Duraid, *Ištiqāq* 170, Ibn Manẓūr, II, 1312, Howell, I, fasc. IV, 1767-1768:

" جَاؤوا بِجَيْشٍ لَوْ قِيسَ مُعْرَسُهم     مَا كَانَ إلا كَمُعْرَسِ الدُّئِلِ " .

*"Ǧā*ᵓ*ū bi-ğayšin law qīsa mu*ᶜ*rasuhum*
*mā kāna* ᵓ*illā ka-mu*ᶜ*rasi l-du*ᵓ*ili".*
"They brought an army such that, if its halting-ground
were measured,
it would be only like the halting ground of the weasel".

<u>*46.1 In verbs with 2nd weak radical:*</u>

In the cases of the passive voice of the perfect *fu*ᶜ*ila* فُعِلَ, the ḍamma precedes the kasra, a fact which brings about some phonological changes.

In verbs with 2nd radical *w,* the *w* is considered as unsound and gives hand to two possibilities.

1st possibility: *-uwi* with the *w* vowelled by a kasra and preceded by a ḍamma becomes *-iw* after that the *w's* kasra is shifted before the *w* and hence the ḍamma is changed into a kasra. As in it the vowelless *w* is preceded by a kasra, the *w* is changed into an *ī:* lengthened *ī,* namely *-iy / (i)ī.*

An example of this sequence is found in a verb with 2nd radical *w* in the passive voice formed according to *fu*$^{c}$*ila* فُعِلَ, e.g. *quwila* قُوِلَ "it was said". According to this theory *quwila* قُوِلَ > *qiwla* قِوْلَ > *q(i)yla* قِيْلَ > *q(i)īla* قِيلَ can be mentioned.

2nd possibility: *-uwi* with the *w* vowelled by a kasra and preceded by a ḍamma becomes *–uw* after that the *w's* kasra is elided for the sake of alleviation. As in it the vowelless *w* is preceded by a ḍamma, the *w* is changed into an *ū:* lengthened *ū* so that it becomes *-(u)ū.* According to this theory the example *quwila* قُوِلَ > *quwla* قُوْلَ > *q(u)ūla* قُولَ can be mentioned.

In verbs with 2nd radical *y,* the *y* is considered as unsound and gives hand to two possibilities.

1st possibility: *-uyi* with the *y* vowelled by a kasra and preceded by a ḍamma becomes *-iy* after that the *y's* kasra is shifted before the *y* and hence the ḍamma is changed into a kasra. As there is in it a vowelless *y* preceded by a kasra the *y* is changed into an *ī:* lengthened *ī,* so that it becomes *(i)ī.*

An example of this sequence is found in a verb with 2nd radical *y* in the passive voice formed according to *fuᶜila* فُعِلَ, e.g. *buyiᶜa* بُيِعَ "it was sold". According to this theory, the changes are the following: *buyiᶜa* بُيِعَ > *biyᶜa* بِيْعَ > *b(i)īᶜa* بِيعَ.

2nd possibility: *-uyi* with the *y* vowelled by a kasra and preceded by a ḍamma becomes *-uy* after that the *y's* kasra is elided for the sake of alleviation. As there is in it a vowelless *y* preceded by a ḍamma, the *y* is changed into a *w,* so that it becomes *-uw.* As there is in it a vowelless *w* preceded by a ḍamma, the *w* is changed into an *ū:* lengthened *ū,* so that it becomes *-(u)ū.* According to this theory the example *buyiᶜa* بُيِعَ > *buyᶜa* بُيْعَ > *b(u)wᶜa* بُوْعَ > *b(u)ūᶜa* بُوعَ can be mentioned.

It can be added that *b(u)ūᶜa* بُوعَ with pure ḍamma occurs in the dialect of the Banū Dubair and the Banū Faḫᶜas. It occurs anomalously instead of *buyiᶜa* بُيِعَ in this verse said by Ruᵓba, cited by Ibn Yaᶜīš, VII, 70, Suyūṭī, *Šarḥ* 277, Šinqīṭī, *Durar I,*

206, II, 222, Daqr, *Muᶜǧam* 389, Howell, II-III, 122, Åkesson, *Ibn Masᶜūd,* the Commentary (298):

"لَيْتَ وَهَلْ يَنْفَعُ شيئاً لَيْتُ          لَيْتَ شبَاباً بُوعَ فَاشتَرَيْتُ".

*"layta wa-hal yanfaᶜu šayᶜan laytu*
*layta šabāban būᶜa fa-štaraytu".*
"Would that - but does a 'would that' profit anything?
Would that youth were sold and that I bought".

## 47- The combination of the kasra preceding the ḍamma is disliked

A rare noun with the disliked combination of the kasra preceding the ḍamma is *ḥibukun* حِبُكٌ formed upon the measure *fiᶜulun* فِعُلٌ with the 1st radical vowelled by a kasra followed by the 2nd vowelled by a ḍamma (cf. Lane, I, 503).

## 48- The combination of the kasras is disliked

<u>*48.1 In a verb with 3rd weak radical y:*</u>

The 2nd radical *m* is vowelled by a fatḥa in the name of place *al-marm(a)ā* الْمَرْمَى "a place of throwing or shooting arrows" that is said instead of *al-marm(i)yu* الْمَرْمِيُ with the last *y* considered as two kasras. The pattern becomes conformable to *maf$^c$alun* مَفْعَلٌ instead of *maf$^c$ilun* مَفْعِلٌ to avoid the combination of the kasras, and so breaks the rule that requires that *ram(a)ā yarmiyu* رَمَى يَرْمِيُ "to throw" is according to the conjugation *fa$^c$ala yaf$^c$ilu* فَعَلَ يَفْعِلُ of which the noun of place should principally be conformable to *maf$^c$ilun* مَفْعِلٌ (cf. Åkesson, *Ibn Mas$^c$ūd,* the Arabic text fols. 16b-17a).

### 49- The fatḥa vowels the *n* of the ending *-īna* of the 2nd person of the fem. sing. of the imperfect of the indicative

The *-na* of the indicative of the 2nd person of the fem. sing. in the ending *–īna,* e.g. *taḍrib(i)īna* تَضْرِبِينَ offers a similarity with the *-na* of the ending *-īna* in nouns that occur in the masc. sound pl. of the accusative, e.g. *ra$^ᵓ$aytu l-ṭ(a)ālib(i)īna* رَأَيْتُ الطَّالِبِينَ "I saw the demanding persons" and of the genitive, e.g. *$^c$inda l-ṭ(a)ālib(i)īna* عِنْدَ الطَّالِبِينَ "by the demanding persons", which is probably the reason why the *n* in *-na* was as well vowelled by a fatḥa (cf. Muᵓaddib, *Taṣrīf* 34). This is why Muᵓaddib (ibid, 35) states that the *n* of *ām(i)īna* أمِينَ "Amen" was as well vowelled by a fatḥa because of its similarity with the *-na* of the ending *-īna* in the sound masc. pl. of nouns.

**50- The kasra vowels the *n* of the ending *–āni* of the duals of the imperfect of the indicative**

The *n* of the imperfect of the indicative of the dual of 2nd person of the masc. and fem. e.g. *taḍrib(a)āni* تَضرِبَانِ, of the 3rd person of the masc. *yaḍrib(a)āni* يَضرِبَانِ and of the 3rd person of the fem. *taḍrib(a)āni* تَضرِبَانِ that follows the *ā,* is given the kasra because of a similarity between it and the *n* of the ending *-āni* of the dual vowelled by a kasra in nouns occurring in the dual of the nominative, e.g. *ṭ(a)ālib(a)āni* طَالِبَانِ "two students".

According to al-Kisāʾī's theory referred to by Muʾaddib, *Taṣrīf* 29-30, the *n* was vowelled by a kasra, because when two vowelless letters of which the 1st one is the weak letter *ā,* are combined together in one word, it is of common usage that the 2nd letter is vowelled by a kasra. Examples are *dar(a)āki* دَرَاكِ "attain you! (an imperative verbal noun meaning *ʾadrik qaṭ(a)āmi* أدْرِكْ قَطَامِ "Qaṭāmi, name of a woman" (cf. Ibn Manẓūr, V, 3682) and *ḥaḏ(a)āmi* خَذَامِ "Ḥaḏāmi, name of a woman" (cf. Ibn Manẓūr, II, 813).

Another theory mentioned by Mu°addib, *Taṣrīf* 30 is that the *n* of the dual of the ending *-āni* انِ is given a kasra to differenciate it from the *n* of the pl. of the ending *–ūna* ونَ that is given a fatḥa.

<u>*50.1 Anomalous cases:*</u>

The *n* of the dual has been given anomalous vowels in nouns (cf. Rabin, 67, Mu°addib, *Taṣrīf* 197, Ibn Ǧinnī, *Taṯniya* 87, Ibn ᶜAqīl, *Musāᶜid* 40, Ibn Yaᶜīš, IV, 143).

An example with the *n* given anomalously a fatḥa in a verb is recorded in *(°ataᶜid(a)ānan(i)ī)* أتَعِدانَنِي read so by Abū ᶜAmr of the sur. 46: 17 instead of *(°ataᶜid(a)ānin(i)ī)* أتَعِدانِنِي "Do you hold out the promise to me" (cf. Ibn Ḫālawaihi, *Qirāʾāt II,* 318).

**51- The kasra vowels the doubled *n* in the duals of the imperfect of the Energetic I**

The reason why the doubled *n* is vowelled by a kasra in the duals of the imperfect of the Energetic I, i.e. the duals of the 2nd person of the masc. and fem. in e.g. *taḍrib(a)ānni* تَضْرِبَانِّ "You both hit" and the dual of the 3rd person of the masc. in e.g. *yaḍrib(a)ānni* يَضْرِبَانِّ "they both hit /masc." and of the fem. in e.g. *taḍrib(a)ānni* تَضْرِبَانِّ "they both hit /fem." is because of its resemblance to the *-ni* of the declinable forms, i.e. the *-ni* of the dual of nouns, e.g. *rağul(a)āni* رَجُلَانِ "two men", and the *-ni* of the imperfect of the indicative of verbs, e.g. *yaḍrib(a)āni* يَضْرِبَانِ "they both hit /masc. dual". It is this *n's* occurrence after the infixed *ā* which made it similar to the *-ni* of the dual occurring after the infixed *ā* (cf. Sībawaihi, II, 160).

**52- The fatḥa vowels the *n* of the ending *–ūna* of the 2nd and 3rd persons of the masc. pl. of the imperfect of the indicative**

The *n* of the 2nd and 3rd persons of the masc. pl. that follows the *w* in e.g. *taḍrib(u)ūna* تَضْرِبُونَ and *yaḍrib(u)ūna* يَضْرِبُونَ offers a similarity with the *n* vowelled by a fatḥa that follows the *ū* in nouns of the masc. sound pl. of the nominative, e.g. *al-Zayd(u)ūna* الزَّيْدُونَ "the Zaids".

According to Abū ᶜAlī's theory reported by Muḥammad b. al-Mustanīr Quṭrub referred to by Muᵓaddib, *Taṣrīf* 30, the reason of vowelling the *n* in nouns of the masc. sound pl. of the nominative with the lightest of vowels, the fatḥa, is to lighten its combination with the heaviest weak letter among the weak letters marking the declension, which is the *w*.

**53- The kasra vowelling the imperfect prefix is heavy**

In the dialectal variants of Qais, Tamīm, Asad, Rabīᶜa and some other Arabs, the imperfect prefix is given a kasra, except when it concerns the 3rd person of the masc. sing. (cf. Rabin,

61), the *ya,* on account of the heaviness of the combination of the *y* and the kasra. An anomalous verb with this vowelling *yiʾb(a)ā* يِئبَى "he refuses" exists however (cf. Åkesson, *Ibn Masʿūd,* the Commentary (32), Wright, II, 93). It seems that this verb with hamza as its 1st radical is made conformable to *yiyǧalu* يِيْجَلُ "he is afraid", a verb with 1st weak radical regarding its integration within the conjugation *faʿila* فَعِلَ and having a *y* that follows the imperfect prefixed *y* (cf. Sībawaihi, II, 276). The vowelling of the *y* imperfect prefix of the 3rd person of the masc. sing. with a kasra takes place in the Quḍāʿa dialects, in Hebrew, Western Aramaic and Ugaritic (cf. Rabin, 61).

# III. BIBLIOGRAPHY

## III.1. Primary sources

ᶜAbd al-Ḥamīd, *Taṣrīf* = ᶜAbd al-Ḥamīd, M. Muḥyī l-Dīn, *Takmila fī Taṣrīf al-afᶜāl,* the work printed after Ibn ᶜAqīl, *Šarḥ II.*

Åkesson, *Ibn Masᶜūd* = Åkesson, J. , *Arabic Morphology and Phonology based on the Marāḥ al-arwāḥ by Aḥmad b. ᶜAlī b. Masᶜūd, Presented with an Introduction, Arabic Edition, English Translation and Commentary,* Leiden 2001.

Ḫalīl b. Aḥmad..., *Ḥurūf* = Ḫalīl b. Aḥmad wa-b. al-Sikkīt wa-l-Rāzī, *Ṯalāṯat kutub fī l-ḥurūf,* Ed. R. ᶜAbd al-Tawwāb, Cairo 1982.

Ibn al-Anbārī, *Inṣāf* = Ibn al-Anbārī, Abū l-Barakāt, *Kitāb al-inṣāf fī masāʾil al-ḫilāf bayna l-naḥwīyīn al-baṣrīyīn wa-l-*

*kūfīyīn: Die grammatischen Schulen von Kufa und Basra,* Ed. G. Weil, Leiden 1913.

Ibn ᶜAqīl = Ibn ᶜAqīl, Bihāʾal-Dīn ᶜAbdallāh, *Šarḥ ᶜalā alfīyat Ibn Mālik,* Ed. M. Muḥyī l-Dīn ᶜAbd al-Ḥamīd, 2 vol., s.a., with *Takmila fī tašrīf al-afᶜāl printed* after it by ᶜAbd al-Ḥamīd, M. Muḥyī l-Dīn ᶜAbd al-Ḥamīd [see ᶜAbd al-Ḥamīd, *Taṣrīf].*

Ibn ᶜAqīl, *Musāᶜid* = Ibn ᶜAqīl, Bihāʾal-Dīn ᶜAbdallāh, *al-Musāᶜid ᶜalā tashīl al-fawāʾid,* Ed. M. Kāmil Barakāt, Damascus 1980.

Ibn Duraid, I*štiqāq* = Ibn Duraid, Abū Bakr Muḥammad b. al-Ḥasan, *al-Ištiqāq,* Ed. ᶜA. S. M. Harūn, Cairo s.a.

Ibn Ǧinnī, *de Flexione* = Ibn Ǧinnîi, Abū l-Fatḥ ᶜUṯmān, *de Flexione Libellvs,* Ed. G. Hoberg, Lipsiae, 1885.

Ibn Ǧinnī, *Ḫaṣāʾiṣ* = Ibn Ǧinnī, Abū l-Fatḥ ᶜUṯmān, *al-Ḫaṣāʾiṣ,* Ed. M. A. al-Naǧǧār, 3 vol., Cairo 1371/1952-1376/1956.

Ibn Ǧinnī, *Munṣif* = Ibn Ǧinnī, Abū l-Fatḥ ᶜUṯmān, *al-Munṣif fī šarḥ taṣrīf al-Māzinī,* Ed. I. Muṣṭafā, ᶜA. Amīn, 3 vol., Cairo 1373/1954-1379/1960.

Ibn Ǧinnī, *Sirr* = Ibn Ǧinnī, Abū l-Fatḥ ᶜUṯmān, *Sirr ṣināᶜat al-iᶜrāb,* Ed. Ḥ. Hindāwī, 2 vol., Damascus 1405/1985.

Ibn Ǧinnī, *Tatniya* = Ibn Ǧinnī, Abū l-Fatḥ ᶜUṯmān, *ᶜIlal al-taṯniya,* Ed. Ṣ. al-Tamīmī and R. ᶜAbd al-Tawwāb, Cairo 1992.

Ibn Ḫālawaihi, *Qirāʾāt* = Ibn Ḫālawaihi, Abū ᶜAbd Allāh al-Ḥusain b. Aḥmad, *Iᶜrāb al-qirāʾāt al-sabᶜ wa-ᶜilaluhā,* Ed. ᶜAbd al-Raḥmān b. Sulaimān al-ᶜAtīmain, 2 vol., Cairo 1413/1992.

Ibn Mālik, *Alfīya* = Ibn Mālik, Muḥammad b. ᶜAbd Allāh, *La ʾAlfiyyah dʾIbnu-Malik* [pp. 1-227], suivie de (->)

Ibn Mālik, *Lāmīya* = Ibn Mālik, Muḥammad b. ᶜAbd Allāh, *La Lâmiyyah* du même auteur [pp. 228-353] avec traduction et notes en français et un lexique des termes techniques par A. Goguyer, Beyrouth 1888.

Ibn Manẓūr = Ibn Manẓūr, Ǧamāl al-Dīn, *Lisān al-ᶜArab,* 6 vol., Beirut undated.

Ibn al-Sarrāǧ, *ʾUṣūl* = Ibn al-Sarrāǧ, Abū Bakr, *al-ʾUṣūl fī l-Naḥw,* Ed. ᶜA. Ḥ. al-Fatlī, Beirut 1408/1988.

Ibn ᶜUṣfūr = Ibn ᶜUṣfūr al-Ašbīlī, Abū l-ᶜAbbās ᶜAlī b. Muʾmin, *al-Mumtiᶜ fī l-taṣrīf,* Ed. F. al-Dīn Qabāwih, Aleppo 1390/1970.

Ibn Yaᶜīš = Ibn Yaᶜīš, Muwaffaq al-Dīn Abū l-Barāʾ Yaᶜīš, *Šarḥ al-mufaṣṣal, 2* vol., Beirut undated.

Ibn Yaᶜīš, *Mulūkī* = Ibn Yaᶜīš, Muwaffaq al-Dīn Abū l-Barāᵓ Yaᶜīš, *Šarḥ al-mulūkī fī l-taṣrīf,* Ed. Faḫr al-Dīn Qabāwa, Aleppo 1393/1973.

Muᵓaddib, *Taṣrīf* = Al-Muᵓaddib, al-Qāsim b. Muḥammad b. Saᶜīd, *Daqāᵓiq al-taṣrīf,* Ed. A. N. al-Qaisī, Ḥ. Ṣ. al-Ḍāmin and Ḥ. Tūrāl, Iraq 1407/1987.

Sībawaihi = Sîbawaihi, Abū Bišr ᶜAmr b. ᶜUṯmān, *Le Livre de Sîbawaihi (Kitāb Sībawaihi), Traité de grammaire arabe,* Ed. H. Derenbourg, 2 vol., Paris 1881-1889. Réimpression: 1970.

Sinqīṭī, *Durar* = Al-Šinqīṭī, Aḥmad b. al-Amīn, *al-Durar al-lawāmiᶜ ᶜalā hamᶜ al-hawāmiᶜ,* 2 vol., Cairo 1328/1910.

Suyūṭī, *Ašbāh* = Al-Suyūtī, Ǧalāl al-Dīn Abū l-Faḍl ᶜAbd al-Raḥmān, *al-ᵓAšbāh wa-l-naẓāᵓir,* Ed. ᶜAbd Allāh Nabhān, 4 vol., Damascus 1406/1985.

Suyūṭī, *Muzhir* = Al-Suyūtī, Ǧalāl al-Dīn Abū l-Faḍl ᶜAbd al-Raḥmān, *al-Muzhir fī ᶜulūm al-luġa wa-anwāᶜihā,* 2 vol., Cairo s.a.

Suyūṭī, *Šarḥ* = Al-Suyūtī, Ǧalāl al-Dīn Abū l-Faḍl ᶜAbd al-Raḥmān, *Šarḥ šawāhid al-muġnī,* Cairo 1322.

Zaǧǧāǧī, *Īḍāḥ* = Al-Zaǧǧāǧī, Abū Qāsim ᶜAbd al-Raḥmān, *al-Īḍāḥ fī ᶜilal al-naḥw,* Ed. M. al-Mubārak, Cairo 1378/1959.

Zaǧǧāǧī, *Maǧālis* = Al-Zaǧǧāǧī, Abū Qāsim ᶜAbd al-Raḥmān, *Maǧālis al-ᶜulamāʾ*, Ed. ᶜA. S. M. Harūn, Kuwait 1962.

Zamaḫšarī = Zamaḫsʾario, Abū l-Qāsim Maḥmūd b. ᶜUmar, *al-Mufaṣṣal,* Ed. J. P. Broch, Christianiae 1840.

## III.2. Secondary sources

ᶜAbd al-Tawwāb, *Taṭawwur* = ᶜAbd al-Tawwāb, Ramaḍān, *al-Taṭawwur al-luġawī, maẓāhiruhu wa-ᶜilaluhu wa-qawanīnuhu,* Cairo 1404/1983.

Åkesson, *Conversion* = Åkesson, J., *Conversion of the yāʾ into an alif in Classical Arabic* in: ZAL 31, Wiesbaden 1996.

Åkesson, *Ibn Masᶜūd* = Åkesson, J., *Arabic Morphology and Phonology based on the Marāḥ al-arwāḥ by Aḥmad b. ᶜAlī b. Masᶜūd, Presented with an Introduction, Arabic Edition, English Translation and Commentary,* Leiden 2001.

Alee, *Wasīṭ* = Alee, Mouluvee Toorab, *Wasīṭ al-naḥw, A treatise on the syntax of the Arabic language,* Madras 1820.

Bohas/Kouloughli, *Linguistic* = Bohas, G., Guillaume, J.-P., Kouloughli, D.E., *The Arabic Linguistic Tradition,* London and New York 1990.

Bohas, *Étude* = Bohas, G., Guillaume, J-P, *Étude des théories des grammairiens arabes,* Damas, 1984.

Cohen, *Études* = Cohen, D., *Études de linguistique sémitique et arabe,* The Hague/Paris 1970.

Daqr, *Mu*ᶜ*ğam* = Daqr, ᶜAbd al-Ġanī, *Mu*ᶜ*ğam al-naḥw,* Beirut 1407 A.H. /1986.

Fleisch, *Traité I* = Fleisch, H., *Traité de Philologie Arabe, vol. I, Préliminaires, Phonétique Morphologie Nominale,* Beyrouth 1961.

Fleisch, *Traité II* = Fleisch, H., *Traité de Philologie Arabe, vol. II, Pronoms, Morphologie verbale, Particules,* Beyrouth 1979.

Ḥassān, *Uṣūl* = Ḥassān, Tammām, *al-Uṣūl,* Cairo 1982.

Hindāwī, *Manāhiğ* = Hindāwī, Ḥasan, *Manāhiğ al-ṣarfīyīn wa-maḏahibuhum fī l-qarnain al-ṯāliṯ wa-l-rābi*ᶜ *mina l-hiğra,* Damascus 1409/1989.

Howell = Howell, M. S., *Grammar of the Classical Arabic Language,* 4 parts in 7 vol., Allahabad 1880-1911.

Lane = Lane, E.W., *Arabic-English Lexicon,* 8 in 2 vol., London 1863-1893. Reprint: 1984.

Nöldeke, *Grammatik* = Nöldeke, T., *Zur Grammatik des Classischen Arabisch im Anhang: Die Handschriftlichen ergänzungen in dem Handexemplar Theodor Nöldekes bearbeitet und mit zuzätzen versehen von Anton Spitaler,* Darmstadt 1963.

O'Leary, *Semitic Languages* = O'Leary, De L., *Comparative Grammar of the Semitic Languages,* London 1923.

Penrice, *Dictionary* = Penrice, J., *A Dictionary and Glossary of the Koran,* London 1873. Reprint: 1971.

Rabin = Rabin, C., Ancient West-Arabian, London 1951.

Roman, *Étude* = Roman, A., *Étude de la phonologie et de la morphologie de la koinè arabe,* 2 vol., Publications de l'Université de Provence, Marseille 1983.

De Sacy = De Sacy, S., *Grammaire arabe,* 2 vol., Tunis 1904-1905.

Talmon, *ᶜAyn* = Talmon, R., *Arabic Grammar in its formative Age, Kitāb al-ᶜAyn and its Attribution to Ḫalīl b. Aḥmad,* Leiden - New York - Køln 1997.

Vernier = Vernier, D., *Grammaire arabe,* 2 vol., Beyrouth 1891.

Versteegh, *Zağğāğī* = Versteegh, K., *The explanation of linguistic causes. Az-Zağğāğī's theory of grammar. Introduction, translation, commentary,* Amsterdam 1995.

Wright = Wright, W., *A Grammar of the Arabic Language,* Cambridge, Third Edition 1985.

Wright, *Comparative Grammar* = Wright, W., *Lectures on the Comparative Grammar of the Semitic Languages,* Cambridge 1890.

# IV. INDEX OF QUR'ANIC QUOTATIONS

| | | | |
|---|---|---|---|
| 20: | 132 | 84 | *(wa-ʾamur ʾahlaka bi-l-ṣalwati)* وَأمُرْ أهلَكَ بالصَلْوَاتِ "Enjoin prayer on thy people". |
| 23: | 1 | 100 | *(qad ʾaflaḥa l-muʾminūna)* قَدَ أفْلَحَ الْمُؤمِنُون "The Believers must (eventually) win through". |
| 29: | 64 | 67 | *(la-hya l-ḥayawānu)* لَهْيَ الْحَيَوَانُ "that is Life indeed". |
| 33: | 33 | 29 | *(wa-qarna fī buyūtikunna)* وَقَرْنَ في بُيُوتكُنّ "You shall settle down in your homes". |
| 42: | 5 | 14 | *(yatafaṭṭarna)* يَتَفَطّرْنَ "Rent asunder". |
| 42: | 5 | 21 | *(yatafaṭṭarna)* يَتَفَطّرْنَ "Rent asunder". |
| 46: | 17 | 111 | *(ʾataʿidāninī)* أتَعِدَانني "Do you hold out the promise to me". |
| 47: | 18 | 87 | *(fa-qad ǧāʾa ʾašrāṭuhā)* فَقَدْ جاءَ أشراطُها "But already Have come some tokens". |
| 56: | 65 | 26 | *(fa-ẓaltum tafakkahūna)* فظَلْتُمْ تَفَكّهُونَ "And ye would be left in wonderment". |
| 73: | 2 | 46 | *(qumu l-layla)* قُمِ ألّيْلَ "Stand (to prayer) by night". |
| 77: | 11 | 8 | *(wa-ʾidā ʾuqqitati r-rusulu)* وَإذَا أُقّتَتِ الرّسُلُ "And when the apostles are (all) appointed a time (to collect); -". |

# V. INDEX OF VERSES

لا تُهِينَ الْفَقِيرِ عَلّكَ تَرْكَع

*Laysa man māta fa-starāḥa bi-maytin* *79-80*

لَيْسَ مَنْ مَاتَ فَاسْتَرَاحَ بِمَيْتٍ

*layta wa-hal yanfa*ᶜ*u šay*ᶜ*an laytu* *108*

لَيْتَ وَهَلْ يَنْفَعُ شيئاً لَيْت

*Rāḥat bi-Maslamata l-biġālu* ᶜ*ašiyyata* *90*

رَاحَتْ بِمَسْلَمَةَ الْبِغَالُ عَشِيّة

*Wa-mā maliltu wa-lākin zāda ḥubbukum* *27*

وَمَا مَلِلْتُ وَلَكِنْ زَادَ حُبُّكُم

*Ẓiltu fīhā ḏāta yawma wāqifan* *27*

ظِلْتُ فِيهَا ذَاتَ يومَ وَاقِفا

## VI. INDEX OF NAMES

www.ingramcontent.com/pod-product-compliance
Lightning Source LLC
LaVergne TN
LVHW011239080426
835509LV00005B/559
* 9 7 8 9 1 9 7 8 9 5 4 3 9 *